THE NEW AMERICAN GARDEN

**Innovations in Residential
Landscape Architecture**

60 Case Studies

THE NEW AMERICAN GARDEN

Innovations in Residential Landscape Architecture

60 Case Studies

Edited by
JAMES GRAYSON TRULOVE

Designed by
JAMES PITTMAN

Whitney Library of Design
an imprint of
Watson-Guptill Publications/New York

Half-title page: Ellison Residence, Ron Herman, landscape architect.
Title page: Gerry and Sandra Goldberg Garden, Dunn Associates.
Opposite foreword: Landscape site plan, Lewis Residence, Floor & Ten Eyck Landscape Architecture.

To Mallory B. Duncan

Editor: Micaela Porta
Designer: James Pittman
Production Manager: Ellen Greene

Published in 1998 by Whitney Library of Design,
an imprint of Watson-Guptill Publications, a division
of BPI Communications, Inc., 1515 Broadway,
New York, NY 10036.

Library of Congress Cataloging-in-Publication Data

The New American garden: innovations in residential
landscape architecture: 60 case studies/edited by
James Grayson Trulove.
  p. cm.
  ISBN 0-8230-3168-3
  1. Gardens—United States—Design—Case studies.
2. Gardens—United States—Pictorial works. 3. Gardens—
United States—Designs and plans. 4. Landscape architecture—United States—Case studies.
I. Trulove, James Grayson.
  SB473.N384 1998
  712'.6'0973—dc21   97-51935
                        CIP

Manufactured in China

First Printing, 1998

2 3 4 5 6 7 8 9 /02 01 00

Contents

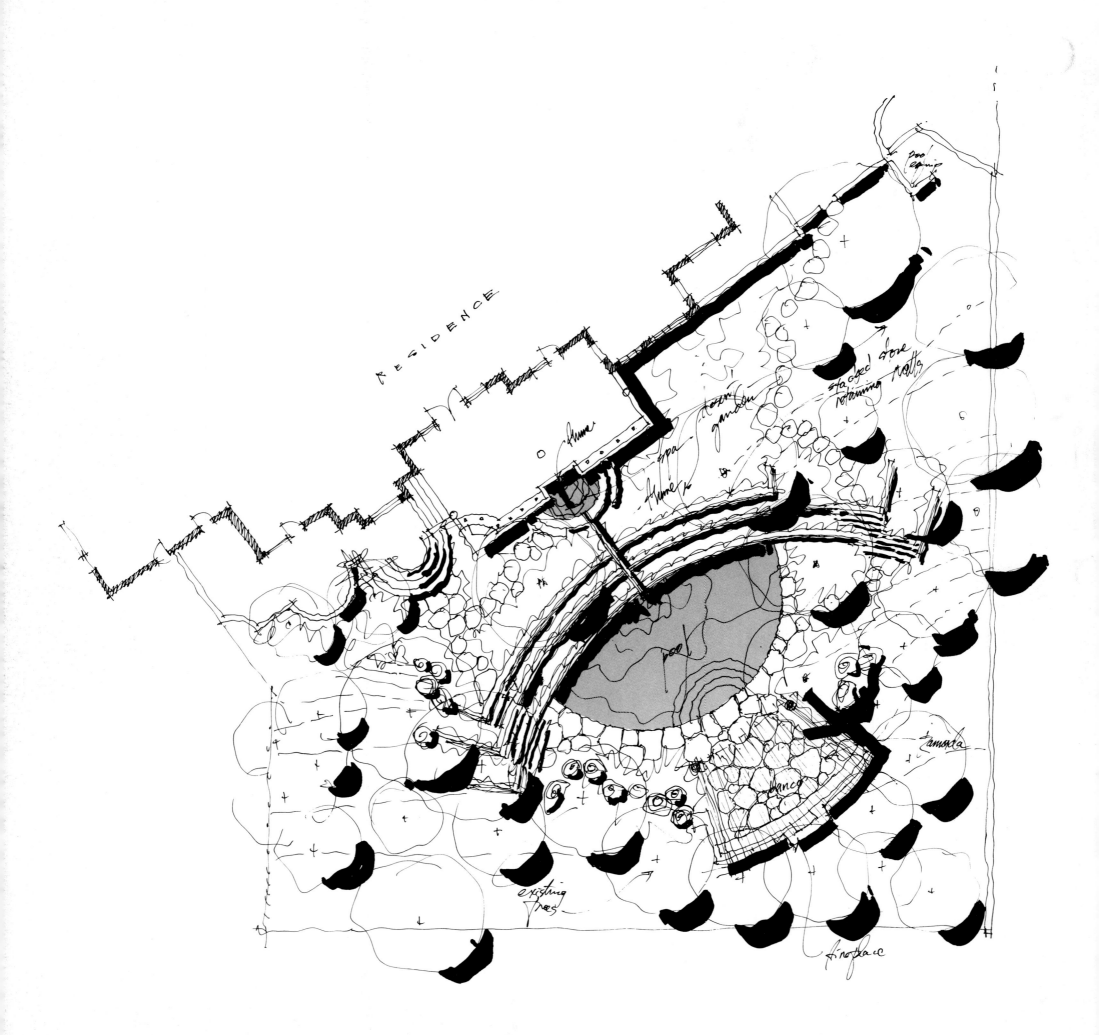

Foreword

Too often the role of the landscape architect is one of solving problems created by poor site selection, bad architecture, or changing living patterns of clients. Rare is the enlightened home builder who chooses the landscape architect before choosing the architect. Who understands the importance of analyzing the entire building site before the foundations are dug rather than afterwards. Who views the two professions as equal partners in a design process that requires just as much attention to the land upon which the house sits as the house itself. And finally, who realizes that just as an architect is chosen for his or her design esthetic, so too should the landscape architect.

The New American Garden was edited with the idea of elevating the importance of the role landscape architecture plays in residential design by presenting the work of twenty-seven of the most creative and successful American landscape architects practicing today. Envisioned as a companion to The New American House, which presents case studies of the residential work of important architects, The New American Garden takes the same case study approach to sixty gardens. Unlike most garden books, it goes beyond just presenting stunning pictures of beautiful gardens. Rather, The New American Garden explores how the gardens were made and under what conditions. Each case study presents the design goals of the landscape architect, the needs of the client, and how the final design met those needs. In most instances, detailed site plans are provided as well as descriptions of major plant and hardscape materials that were used and the prevailing soils and climatic conditions.

Choosing the landscape architects and their work for this book was a daunting task and the final selections are by no means conclusive. Viewed collectively however, the reader should come away with a much clearer understanding of the extraordinarily vital and creative forces that are the underpinnings of today's American residential landscape architecture. The book presents a broad range of design styles from the whimsical to the intellectual, from the avant-garde to the traditional.

While landscape architects often do not have the widespread name recognition that those in other design professions do, many of the landscape architects presented in this volume have a substantial and loyal following both nationally and internationally. Some are senior practitioners whose work has been extensively covered in magazines and books, while others are still developing their practice. All are responsible for creating gardens that should provide inspiration and serve as a valuable reference for those who appreciate the designed landscape.

James Grayson Trulove

Pamela Burton

MALIBU PHOENIX

Location: Malibu, California
Date of Completion: 1996
Owners: Kenneth and Jeanette Chiate
Landscape Architect: Pamela Burton & Company, 2324 Michigan Ave., Santa Monica, CA 90404
Design Team: Pamela Burton, Mary Sager, Sasha Tarnopolsky, Melinda Wood, Jeanette Chiate
Architect: Daly, Genik Architecture
General Contractor: Tyler Development Corporation
Landscape Contractor: Kiralla & Clark
Consultants: Malibu Colony Pool & Spa, Lee Anderson Concrete
Lighting: Pat Skinner
Photography: John Reed Forsman
Site Description: A wide expansive site at the top of a bluff overlooking the Pacific Ocean
Soils: Basalt, Chico conglomerate, standard garden soil
USDA Plant Hardiness Zone: 2
Major Plant Materials: *Olea europaea* (olive), *Schinus molle* (California pepper), *Agonis flexuosa* (peppermint tree), *Aloe stricta, Agave victoriae reginae, Agave vilmoriniana* (octopus agave), *Agave attenuata,* Echeveria, Cotyledon, Artemisia, Cereus, *Anigozanthos fluvidus* (kangaroo paw), *Helictotrichon sempervirens* (blue oat grass), *Plecostachys serpyllifolia, Linum* (flax)
Major Hardscape Materials: Concrete terrace paving with a troweled finish of black silicone carbonate, gravel driveway, and plastered concrete seating walls. The existing brick-edged pool was resurfaced in sky-colored concrete and cut away to form an infinity pool (an open-ended water spill which flows into a catch pool and is recirculated) that merges the pool with the ocean and sky.
Lighting: Fiberoptic tube pool lighting, Kim microflood uplights, Lumiere path lights, uplights.
Building Description: A 1970s ranch house was constructed at odd angles to maximize the ocean view. The house was reconstructed after the Malibu fires into a modern, spare, and elegant set of interior spaces.
Program: The initial program was a simple renovation of the existing brick patio and pool. The original "suburban garden" was replaced with a palette of dramatic succulents and native materials. Gradually, the owners became convinced that the "used" brick finishes related to a past conception of the house—a past which no longer suited the exotic new landscape and house that were emerging.

Right: View south from entry court with mature olive tree.
Below: Landscape site plan.
Far right: Gate leading to pool area.

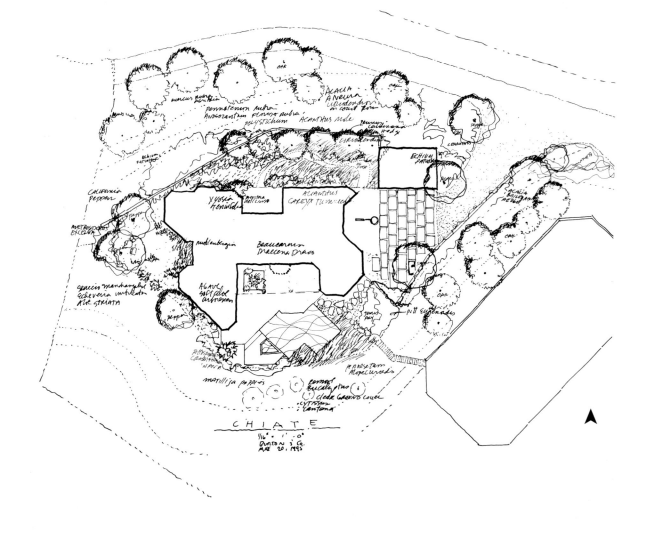

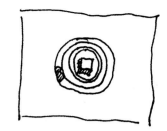

Design

The design attempts to acknowledge the power and beauty of the site's spectacular setting, the sweeping ocean and mountain views, the winds, and sunsets. In the fall of 1993, firestorms swept though the hillsides of Malibu and destroyed many homes, including the one on this site. Though the owners rebuilt the house on the same footing, they completely transformed the original setting to create a seamlessness between the ocean and the sky.

The existing pool was reworked in order to blur the edges between the site and the expansive views, uniting the ocean and the water edge of the pool. A light green-gray concrete pool terrace was poured, seeded with a fine grained black silicone carbonate, then troweled to a smooth finish. The effect is a uniform, shimmering surface.

The pool terrace is framed by masses of blue and green sedum, aloe, cerastium, and kangaroo paw while dramatic euphorbia and agave punctuate the luminescent horizon. Due to the constant movement of the earth and ever-present drainage problems in this part of Malibu, the surface of the long driveway and entry court became an issue. The solution was to cover the existing cracked asphalt with a tack coat and apply a permeable, slate colored gravel. Mature Mission olives, burgundy smoke bushes, agaves, euphorbia, and grasses complete the entry court.

Dominant use of succulents, grasses, and mature olive trees contribute to a low-water plant palette which is sustainable.

an empty
vessel sits
against
a Horizon
of water…
pacific
ocean
Blue

a perfect
circle only
reminded of.
its grounding
By a rock That
couldn't be removed
during construction
That protrudes
into its side
The bottom Holds
a base support
for The roof

A Rundo
Donax makes
the wind
Broom re-appear
in my memory
The way it would
sweep the earth
clean like a chicken
Taking a dust Bath

The mantle revealed

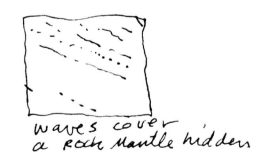

waves cover
a rock mantle hidden

Bushes of
Rhus ovata claim
an eroded cliff

Right, clockwise from top:
Pool merges with the sky and
ocean; *Parodia cacti;*
Trichocereus cacti.

LAKESIDE RETREAT

Location: Toluca Lake, California
Date of Completion: 1995
Owners: Peter and Rosemary Casey
Landscape Architect: Pamela Burton & Company
Design Team: Pamela Burton, Melinda Wood, Sasha Tarnopolsky, David Hardister, Robin Benezra, Katherine Spitz, Joe Desousa
Architect: Thane Roberts Architects
General Contractor: Davis Development Group
Consultants: Carolyn M. Lawrence (architectural interior designs), RBA Partners (civil engineer)
Photography: Sasha Tarnopolsky, Pamela Burton
Site Description: A lakeside garden
Soils: Bedrock, standard garden soil
USDA Plant Hardiness Zone: 2
Major Plant Materials: *Platanus racemosa* (California sycamore), *Schinus molle* (California pepper), *Pyrus calleryana* (ornamental pear), Antique roses, *Achillea millefolium* (yarrow), *Leonotis leonurus* (lion's tail), *Phlomis fruticosa* (Jerusalem sage), *Iris douglasiana* (Douglas iris), *Ceonothus, Buddleia Petite Indigo 'Mongo', Fremontodendron californicum* (Flannel bush), *Lavatera 'Barnsley', Romneya coulteri* (Matilija poppy), *Echinacea purpurea* (purple cone flower)

Right: Landscape site plan. **Below:** View of the stairs down to the lake. **Below right:** Front entry. **Far right:** Stone steps to lake planted with lawn and *Erodium chamaedryoides.*

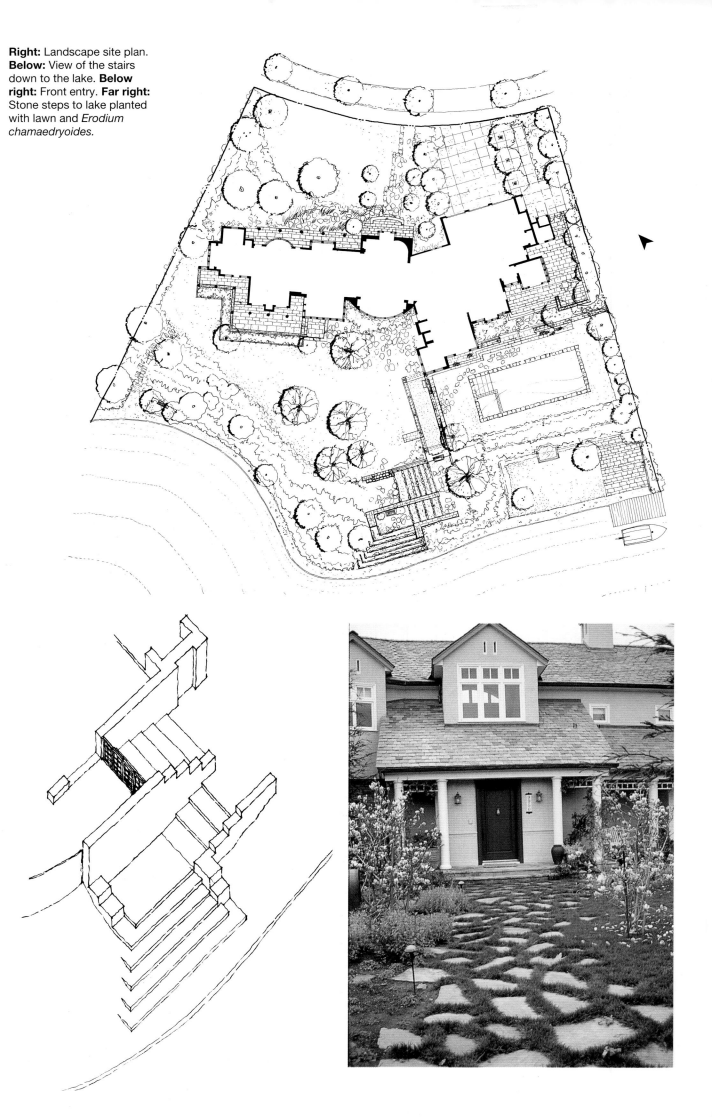

Right, clockwise from top:
Pool fencing is achieved with
a stone curb and plated pergola; view of pool area and
pergola; pool side steps planted with *Lavandula multifida*
and *Erigeron karvinskianus*
(Santa Barbara daisy).

Major Hardscape Materials: Bouquet Canyon, Santa Rita,
and Santa Maria stone pavers, decomposed granite paths,
stone walls, wood pergola, and pool fence.

Program: A busy family with three small children requested
a tranquil garden on the banks of Toluca Lake. Plant
materials and garden elements were used to structure the
site for its many uses and to provide safe areas for the
children to play.

Design

The house opens onto a grand lawn bordered by flowering
perennials. Along one side, a rose-covered pergola forms a
gate to the landscaped pool area. Stone pathways step down
in terraces to a lower lawn and garden at the lakeside. From
here, a decomposed granite path leads to a quiet seating
area. Specimen sycamore and redwood trees mingle with
majestic existing sycamores to give the impression of a
house comfortably settled into its site.

The plant palette was developed to be sustainable through
the use of drought tolerant plants.

Below: Detail of pergola elevation. **Right:** View of planted hill from lakeside.

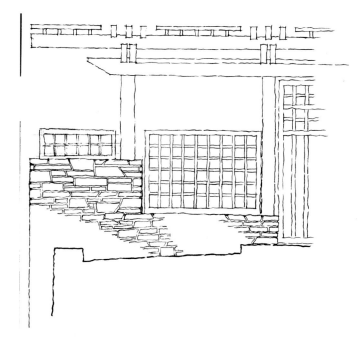

EPIC GARDEN

Below: View of dry stone and hedges forming a room.
Bottom: Landscape site plan.
Right: Entry drive and gate.

Location: Brentwood, California
Date of Completion: 1985
Owner: Gil Friesen
Landscape Architect: Pamela Burton & Company
Design Team: Pamela Burton, John Coplan, Robin Benezera, Susan Costello, Gary Weiss, Sasha Tarnopolsky
Architect: Michael Palladino
General Contractor: Macon Construction (masonry), Arya Construction (general contractor), David Bejelac and Harmony Landscape (landscape contractors)
Photography: Michael Moran, Pamela Burton
Site Description: This site is located in a hillside area of Brentwood in Los Angeles
Soils: Santa Monica shale, clay
USDA Plant Hardiness Zone: 2
Major Plant Materials: *Prunus caroliniana* (Carolina Laurel), *Melaleuca leucadendron* (river tea tree), *Erythrina coralloides* (cherry coral tree), *Liquidambar styraciflua* (American sweet gum), *Cinnamomum camphora* (camphor tree)
Major Hardscape Materials: Bouquet Canyon stone, black granite, gravel
Program: To create a garden that would accommodate the client's outdoor sculpture collection

Design

This garden is based on a series of outdoor rooms, linked by an axial, stepped walk. The walkway is bordered on both sides by symbolic representations of mass and void; the "void" of an empty lawn room, and the "mass" of a citrus orchard. The hedges that define the walk are formed from a native California plant material, *Prunus caroliniana* (Carolina laurel cherry).

At the entrance to the garden from the porch above, one can see the overall layout and the direction of the axial walk. Once inside the garden however, the hedges are like peripheral curtains opening only at certain points to reveal sequentially each separate room. This walk terminates on axis opposite the entrance at a small seating area framed by two urns.

The open lawn has become a badminton court which is defined by two types of sod lawn. The proportions of this open "void" are framed by the axial walk, a columned row of camphor trees, and a low, dry mortar stone wall.

A courtyard for the office is comprised of randomly shaped paving stones in the form of a perfect square around an existing coral tree.

Over time, the owner's interest in collecting contemporary art has grown and the collection has become well represented in the garden. Although not originally designed

Below: Plan of the new vegetable garden adjacent to sculptor Richard Long's *Hollywood Circle*. **Top right:** Sculptor Richard Serra's *Untitled*. **Bottom right:** Richard Long's *Hollywood Circle*.

as a sculpture garden, large-scale pieces such as Richard Long's *Hollywood Circle* (1991) and a work by Richard Serra, *Untitled*, were created specifically for this garden, bringing the garden and art objects together as one contemporary cultural space.

The idea of this garden as a site of contemporary art work is continually inspiring further additions. Recently, a garden folly designed by architect Michael Palladino has become the focus of a graphic, modernist vegetable garden; while Robert Therrien and Jenny Holzer have works installed at the pool area.

The total effect of the garden is of a comfortable yet grand landscape which functions as a subtle backdrop for the artwork while still investigating questions of mass, layering, and void within the landscape.

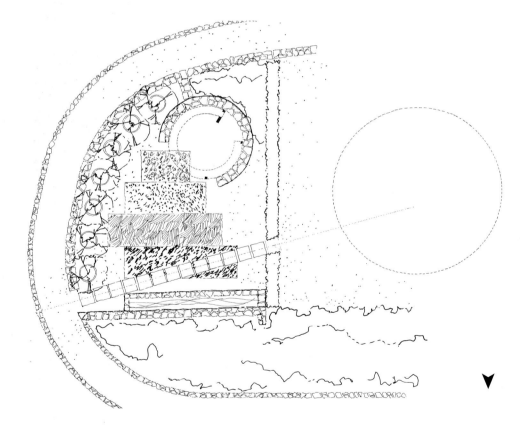

Right, from top: View of the swimming pool with Jenny Holzer bench at far end; urns and bench terminate axis; garden niche. **Below:** Axial stone stair. **Bottom:** Journal sketches.

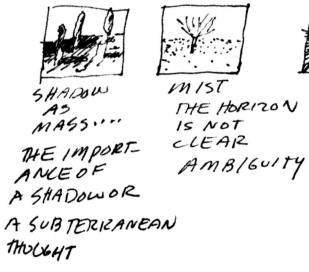

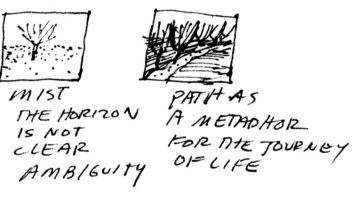

SHADOW AS MASS....

THE IMPORTANCE OF A SHADOW OR A SUBTERRANEAN THOUGHT

MIST THE HORIZON IS NOT CLEAR AMBIGUITY

PATH AS A METAPHOR FOR THE JOURNEY OF LIFE

GARDEN OF THE CHEROKEE ROSE

Location: Brentwood, California
Date of Completion: 1991
Owners: Withheld at client's request.
Landscape Architect: Pamela Burton & Company
Design Team: Pamela Burton, Melinda Wood, Robin Benezra, Sarah Jones, Katherine Spitz, Kirsten Leitner
General Contractor: Linda Yanetty
Photography: Steven Gunther, Michael Moran
Site Description: A back yard garden designed around a climbing Cherokee rose planted in 1906
Soils: Alluvium, standard garden soil
USDA Plant Hardiness Zone: 2
Major Plant Materials: *Platanus racemosa* (California sycamore), *Schinus molle* (California pepper), *Sophora japonica* (Japanese pagoda tree), *Macadamia terrifolia* (Macadamia Nut), *Thalictrum* 'Hewitt's Double', *Carpenteria californica* (Bush Anemone), hybrid tea roses, *Hydrangea macrophylla* 'Tricolor' (variegated garden hydrangea), *Erigeron karvinskianus* (Santa Barbara daisy), *Geranium sanguineum* (cranesbill)
Major Hardscape Materials: Ashlar limestone pavers, Santa Rita and Santa Maria for walls, decomposed granite paths
Lighting: Kim microflood uplights, Lumiere path lights and uplights
Program: The garden was designed to accommodate the client's desire for flowers and outdoor entertaining areas.

Design

This backyard garden in Brentwood is designed around a climbing rose planted in 1906. Since Los Angeles is a city well known for its celebration of the future and not for reverence for the past, the opportunity to canonize a piece of history became the important conceptual principle. A new pergola for this ancient Cherokee rose organizes the

Right: Stone path with pergola and Cherokee rose.
Below: Landscape site plan.

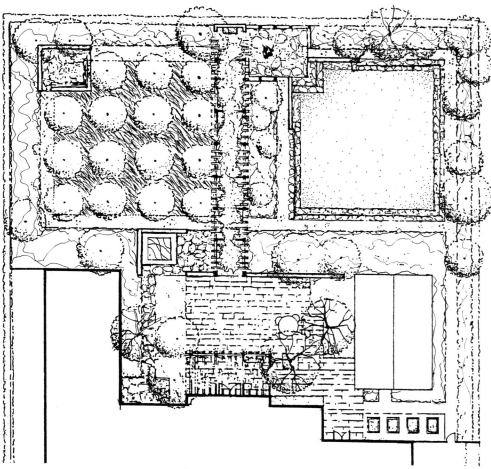

Above: Trunks of the rose
with new supporting posts.
Top right: The recessed lawn
framed with planted steps.
Right: The rose before
construction.

garden into two rooms and provides a strong orientation for
the other garden spaces to accommodate the client's desire
for flowers and outdoor entertaining areas. The pergola
separates the volume into a double square of open spaces:
one a recessed lawn, the other a grove of fruit trees.

The recessed lawn square is shaped with planted steps that
form the edge of a decomposed granite walk. This walk was
intended as a meditation ritual pathway encircling the
entire garden.

The grove of fruit trees was planted with "plumcots," a
hybrid fruit tree of plums crossed with apricots, developed
by the owner's son. The owner himself has been involved in
agriculture in California's Central Valley for over thirty
years.

*Pamela Burton is one of the leaders in a new wave of designers
who are rethinking the role of landscape architecture in
California. In her practice she
combines an extensive
knowledge of plant material,
the history of landscape,
architectural spaces, and fine
arts. Her work has been
featured in major publications.
She teaches at Southern
California Institute of
Architecture and lectures
internationally.*

Above: Pergola separates orchard and spa from recessed lawn. **Right:** Recessed lawn framed by pergola and decomposed granite paths.

A.E. Bye

GAINESWAY FARM

Location: Lexington, Kentucky
Date of Completion: 1983
Owners: Mr. and Mrs. Graham J. Beck
Landscape Architect: A.E. Bye Landscape Architecture, 158 Danbury Road, Ridgefield, CT 06877
Architect: Theodore Ceraldi
Photography: A. E. Bye
Site Description: The house and garden are in the middle of a five-hundred acre farm. The garden overlooks a river and a man-made lake designed by the landscape architect.
Soils: Thin layer of rich soils over limestone.
USDA Plant Hardiness Zone: 6
Major Plant Materials: Oaks, sweet gum, American beech, European beech, weeping European beech, yellow wood, holly, dogwood, yew, purple leaf, winter creeper
Major Hardscape Materials: Local fieldstone, salvaged stone from a distant building site, brick for all walkways
Building Description: A barn converted into a dwelling.
Program: The clients gave the landscape architect great freedom to make a garden that is both highly creative in its design while providing entertaining and viewing areas under large oak trees offering ample shade from the hot summer weather.

Right: View of the ha-ha.
Below: The 450 foot serpentine wall, or ha-ha, was established to eliminate an intrusive fence that stretched across the middle of a pasture to the east of the residence creating a visual interruption of the pasture. **Far right:** The undulations across the landscape were formed to enliven an otherwise plain meadow below the residence. Long low mounds and valleys were sculptured with bulldozers, always keeping in mind positive drainage and ease of mowing the grass. The landscape architect looked to the nearby hilltops for the proper profiles of the mounds.

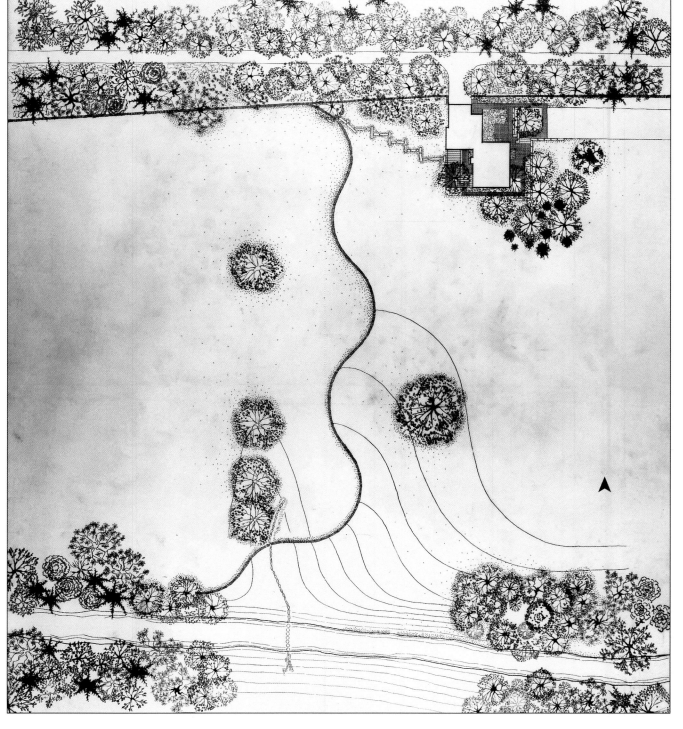

Location: Lexington, Kentucky
Date of Completion: 1983
Owners: John and Joan Gaines
Landscape Architect: A.E. Bye Landscape Architecture, 158 Danbury Road, Ridgefield, CT 06877
Architect: Theodore Ceraldi
Photography: A. E. Bye
Site Description: The house and garden are in the middle of a five-hundred acre farm. The garden overlooks a river and a man-made lake designed by the landscape architect.
Soils: Thin layer of rich soils over limestone.
USDA Plant Hardiness Zone: 6
Major Plant Materials: Oaks, sweet gum, American beech, European beech, weeping European beech, yellow wood, holly, dogwood, yew, purple leaf, winter creeper
Major Hardscape Materials: Local fieldstone, salvaged stone from a distant building site, brick for all walkways
Building Description: A barn converted into a dwelling.
Program: The clients gave the landscape architect great freedom to make a garden that is both highly creative in its design while providing entertaining and viewing areas under large oak trees offering ample shade from the hot summer weather.

A.E. Bye is one of the most prominent landscape architects practicing today. He is known especially for his work at Gainesway Farm and for numerous other residential commissions, such as the Leitzsch Residence in Ridgefield, CT and the Residence on the Connecticut Coast, in Stonington, CT. He is an educator who has taught at the Cooper Union, Columbia University, Pratt Institute, and the University of Pennsylvania. His landscape photographs have become equally well known and have been published extensively. His work with the natural landscape dates to the early 1950s when he worked on a landscape commission for a Frank Lloyd Wright house in Westchester County, NY. Forty years later he continues to work with great sensitivity with natural ecologies.

Top left: An ancient white oak (*Quercus alba*) was isolated from nearby intrusive trees so that its grandeur and sculptural quality could be enjoyed. This tree is also to be admired as a statement of persistence, tenacity, and endurance in old age. **Bottom left:** Although melting snow patterns are unpredictable, they can be enjoyed for the abstractions they create on open lawns and fields when the warmer weather of late winter melts the snow unevenly.
Right: This zigzag stepping stone walk was built in one day, without the benefit of plans. It is an example of spontaneity in design and has proved to be delightful to the child who prances up and down to challenge his balance and dexterity.

Dean Cardasis

PLASTIC GARDEN

Below: Landscape site plan.
Right: The character of the garden's irregular spaces is further defined by the Plexiglass panels which whimsically extend the vinyl-sided edges of the house and engage the plants, stone, and wood.

Location: Northampton, Massachusetts
Date of Completion: 1994
Owners: Withheld at client's request.
Landscape Architect: Dean Cardasis & Associates,
32 Cosby Avenue, Amherst, MA 01002
Design Team: Dean Cardasis
General Contractor: Dean Cardasis
Photography: Dean Cardasis
Site Description: In a landscape, while the "canvas" may be bleak, it is never blank. Except for the animation of numerous children, this suburban neighborhood is bland and spiritless, a utilitarian subdivision in which the existing forest was clear-cut to a uniform depth behind equally set-back houses on half-acre lots. The result was continuous corridors of space with no privacy between the houses and the forest.
Soils: Disturbed
USDA Plant Hardiness Zone: 4
Major Plant Materials: Indigenous
Major Hardscape Materials: Gravel, stone, Plexiglas, wood
Building Description: The house, clad in vinyl with few windows or doors, conceived with little regard to its site, sat upon the opened land like an abandoned plastic toy.
Program: The concept developed by the landscape architect was to bring the razed woodland back to the house and hollow out of it three irregular descending terraced spaces, each flowing from the interior spaces of the dwelling; and to reach out from the "plastic" house with playful, light-transforming, plastic panels which would engage the plants, stone, and wood.

Design

The static patterns of the neighborhood are in counterpoint to the complex and playful spatial geometry of the garden. An ironic balance is achieved between the "plastic" house and its site.

This garden is as lively and playful as the neighborhood children, while also serving the adults' need for private and useful living space on its terraces. Both synthetic (derived

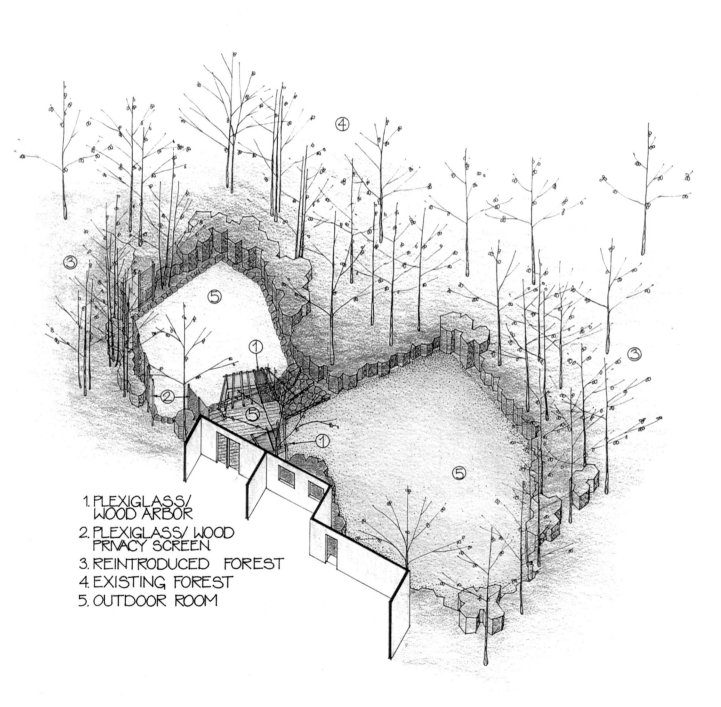

1. PLEXIGLASS/ WOOD ARBOR
2. PLEXIGLASS/ WOOD PRIVACY SCREEN
3. REINTRODUCED FOREST
4. EXISTING FOREST
5. OUTDOOR ROOM

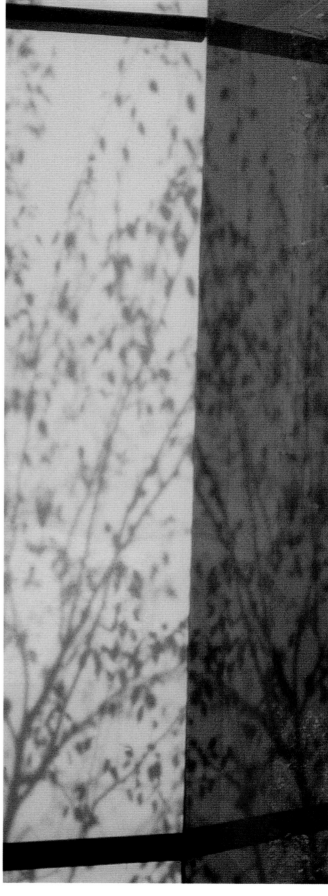

from the house) and "natural" (derived from the woods) materials play with the light and are used as edges to the terraces, creating volumes which have a distinct contemporary quality. Wooden structures are assembled like "pick-up sticks" made out of simple and inexpensive dimension lumber. This plastic garden is a kind of wacky colored origami into which one enters. The experience unfolds within the garden, redefining the outer context of the woods, subdivision, and even the sky by coloring, blocking, and/or silhouetting them, forming an inspiring, useful spatial experience for the family and for the children who play here. This project is based upon a simple contemporary contextual idea: Plastic House/Plastic Garden. But most of all, Plastic Garden is a designed space on a particular piece of land, a unique kind of landscape enclosure, a garden.

Native, indigenous plants that interact with the plastic structures and are an extension of the woodland were selected and the forest encouraged to re-establish itself around the garden. This creates an extremely low-maintenance, sustainable garden. Revealing the future evolution of the forest over the years (as well as seasonally and daily) in relation to the transforming plastic materials is integral to the concept for this garden.

Besides his professional practice, Dean Cardasis is a professor of landscape architecture and director of the James Rose Landscape Research Center. His firm specializes in private gardens as well as public parks and plazas. Cardasis' work has been recognized with awards from the American Society of Landscape Architects and has been published in several books and periodicals.

Right: The sometimes blue ceiling over the dining area of the deck polarizes light and redefines the sky. **Below:** Landscape site plan.

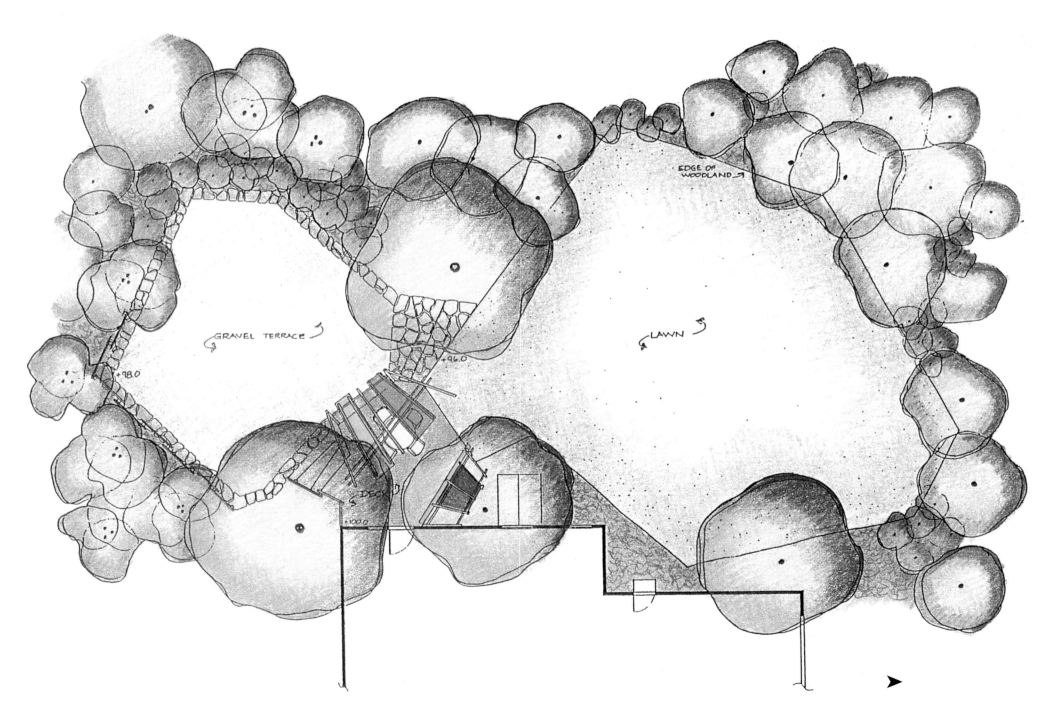

EDGE OF WOODLAND

GRAVEL TERRACE

LAWN

+98.0

+96.0

DECK

+100.0

Jack Chandler

LONG MEADOW RANCH

Location: Napa Valley, California
Date of Completion: 1996
Owners: Withheld at client's request.
Landscape Architect: Jack Chandler & Associates, P.O. Box 2180, Yountville, CA 94599
Design Team: Jack Chandler, ASLA (designer and sculptor), Jennifer Chandler (project landscape architect), Chris Moore, ASLA (project manager)
General Contractor: Owner/builder
Consultants: Ken Campbell (structural engineer)
Photography: Andrew McKinney, Jared Chandler, Jennifer Chandler
Site Description: The surrounding property includes vineyards, a producing olive grove, sheep, and horses, and acres of undisturbed native vegetation, with deer, coyote, and other wildlife. The site itself is very rocky, with lots of rock outcroppings and boulders strewn about.
Soils: Rocky, porous
USDA Plant Hardiness Zone: 8.
Major Plant Materials: Olives, lavender, teucrium, daylilies, Iceberg roses, nepeta
Major Hardscape Materials: Cast stone, concrete paving, native boulders, fieldstone walls, reclaimed timber
Lighting: BK and Coe fixtures.
Building Description: Built in the 1920s by the owner of a local quarry, the house is located high above California's Napa Valley and has a very European country feel with stone arches and columns, red tile roof, and steel shutters.
Program: Despite the incredible view and lovely surroundings, there was little outdoor space for relaxing other than an existing pool and pool deck. The client engaged the landscape architect to create a space for outdoor entertaining and games, including chess, ping-pong, tennis, swimming, and horseshoes. In the process, other areas around the house were refined and beautified.

Design

The landscape architect began by redesigning the auto entry and adding a guest parking area. The existing entry to the house was undistinguished, with one small planting bed and the asphalt drive running up to the edge of the foundation. A series of planting terraces were added using walls made of stone gathered on site and indigenous boulders were incorporated into the steps and walls. Eight thirty-foot olive trees were moved from the olive grove a quarter of a mile away into the planting terraces and surrounding the auto court. A twenty-four inch wall was added at the southwest side of the auto court to contain the space. The wall includes a horse trough/hitching post that doubles as a small fountain. Small niche lights were integrated into the steps and walls to provide soft, unobtrusive, and inviting lighting.

Far right: Looking over the outdoor chess board towards the outdoor dining area.
Right: Main entrance to the house from the parking area.
Bottom: Landscape site plan.

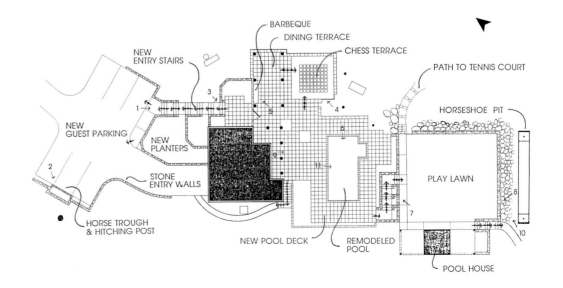

Right top: View towards the outdoor dining area from the pool. **Right bottom:** Main entrance to the house. **Far right:** View over the pool looking towards the long meadow.

At the top of the steps is the front door. A gate, designed by the landscape architect, and a five-foot wall add privacy and a sense of entry to the garden behind. The walls and paving in the garden area closest to the house were designed to echo the stone used to build the house.

Beyond the entry wall, the upper terrace next to the house was expanded to create an outdoor dining room with a barbecue/kitchen sheltered by a pergola. Constructed of recycled and resawn timbers salvaged from an old train station, the pergola will eventually be covered in grape vines. Measurements were taken of the existing house columns and molds were made so that they could be duplicated in cast stone for the pergola columns. Lighting around the terrace was designed to be soft and pleasant and not visible from the valley below. The existing pool was replastered and tiled so it would have a more reflective quality.

Off the outdoor dining area is a small amphitheater with a larger than life metal chess set, designed and fabricated by the landscape architect. Below the main pool terrace is a lawn play terrace surrounded by a stone seat wall. Adjoining is a new pool house designed by the landscape architect to match the main house. The cast stone terrace adjoining the pool house doubles as a ping-pong game room. Below the pool house sits a horseshoe pit. A hand-dug path with stone steps leads down from the lower terrace to the tennis court which is hidden from the house and other view points.

Native monkey flower and sages were planted around the court, and a native grass and wildflower mixture was seeded on all disturbed areas. The planting around the main part of the garden was done in soft Mediterranean perennials and shrub roses to soften the walls and paving. A specimen California live oak anchors the planting area adjacent to the pool. Lavender, rosemary, thyme, and other herbs supply the kitchen. The citrus, roses, and star jasmine add fragrance to the garden. Native deer resistant plants such as *Ceonothus* 'Julia Phelps' and Matilija poppy are used on the outer edges of the garden, easing it into the surrounding landscape.

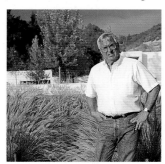

Jack Chandler is a landscape architect and sculptor and principal of Jack Chandler and Associates, in Napa Valley, California. His work as a sculptor has been exhibited throughout California, and his work as a landscape architect has been widely published. He holds a degree in landscape architecture from California State Polytechnic College.

Susan F. Child

RICHMOND GARDEN

Location: Richmond, Massachusetts
Date of Completion: 1987
Owners: Withheld at client's request.
Landscape Architect: Child Associates, Inc. Landscape Architecture, 240 Newbury Street, Boston, MA 02116
Design Team: Susan F. Child (principal-in-charge), Douglas Reed, Anita Berrizbeitia, Toru Mitani
General Contractor: Wendover Farms, Old Chatham, New York
Photography: Cymie Payne, Child Associates, Inc.
Site Description: A fifty-acre property in the Berkshires was composed of three disconnected elements: a Shaker farmhouse, a mountain, and a water-filled quarry.
Soils: Clay, alkaline
USDA Plant Hardiness Zone: 4
Major Plant Materials: *Acer saccharum* (sugar maple), *Betula papyrifera* (paper birch), *Carya ovata* (shagbark hickory), *Juglans nigra* (black walnut), *Malus* sp. (apple), *Populus tremuloides* (quaking aspen), *Prunus* (cherry), *Pyrus* sp. (pear), *Achillea* 'Moonshine' (yarrow), *Anethum graveolens* (dill), *Geranium wallichianum* (geranium 'Buxton Blue'), *Rudbeckia fulgida goldstrum*, *Teucrium chamaedrys* (wall germander)
Major Hardscape Materials: Fieldstone, brick
Program: A coherent environmental design of the site was achieved by sculpting the intervening land into wide lawn and meadow terraces held in place at grade by low fieldstone retaining walls. The terraces are connected with lawn and fieldstone ramps which merge easily one into the other.

Design

The design is simple and spare, recalling the geometry and economy of early Shaker farmsteads and agrarian patterns of the region. The sole adornments of the landscape are grids of orchard trees, brick terraces laid in the designs of early Shaker quilts, and a few native specimen nut trees which punctuate the landscape with shade.

The pleasure of this garden lies in its harmony with the larger Berkshire landscape. While Shaker-inspired in the simplicity of its ground plane and the geometry of its structure, the space of the garden is neither static nor self-contained, as in early Shaker precedents, but moves out freely from terrace to terrace over the landscape—reaching from house, to mountain, to quarry on a grand environmental scale.

Below: Site model/plan.
Bottom: View of the Shaker house, fieldstone retaining wall, and lawn terrace from the road.
Right: Lawn ramps, retained by fieldstone walls at grade, lead from lawn and meadow terraces out to the quarry and the larger landscape.

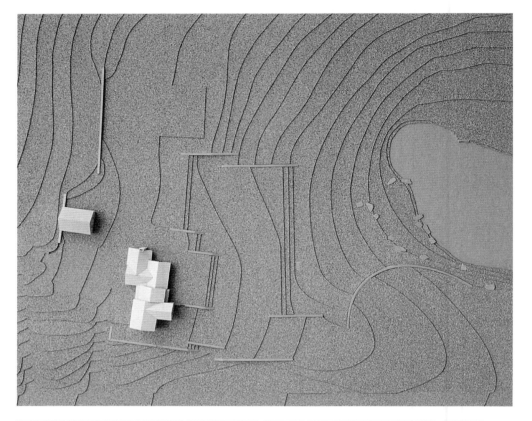

Left: A native specimen tree frames a view across field-stone walls to the quarry and the mountain beyond. **Below:** Site model/elevation. **Right top:** View from the house across a lawn and brick terrace laid in the pattern of a Shaker quilt and bordered with herbs. **Right bottom:** Beneath a wide-spreading native butternut tree, Adirondack chairs afford a view of the meadow, terraced orchard, and quarry pond beyond.

NANTUCKET RESIDENCE

Location: Nantucket, Massachusetts
Date of Completion: 1991
Owners: Withheld at client's request.
Landscape Architect: Child Associates, Inc.
Design Team: Susan F. Child (principal-in-charge),
Douglas Reed, Anita Berrizbeitia
Architect: Edward O'Toole
General Contractor: C.A. Dragon Landscaping,
Nantucket, MA
Photography: Charles Mayer
Site Description: A gray shingle cottage on a small
rectangular lot on a side lane with neighboring cottages on
three sides and the native moor on the fourth.
Soils: Sandy, acid
USDA Plant Hardiness Zone: 6
Major Plant Materials: *Ilex meserveae* (blue holly),
Ligustrum obtusifolium (privet), *Hydrangea mariesii* (lace cap
hydrangea), *Hydrangea paniculata* (Pee Gee hydrangea),
Syringa vulgaris (lilac), *Sophora japonica* (Japanese pagoda
tree), *Malus sp.* (crabapple), *Pyrus* (pear), *Myrica
pennsylvanica* (bayberry), *Rosa rugosa* (Rugosa rose),
Vaccinium angustifolium (lowbush blueberry), *Vaccinium
coymbosum* (highbush blueberry), *Amelanchier canadensis*
(shad), *Nyssa sylvatica* (tupelo), *Clethra alnifolia*
(summersweet), *Ilex opaca* (American holly), *Ilex verticillata*
(winterberry), *Viburnum dentatum* (arrowood viburnum)
Major Hardscape Material: Brick
Program: This Nantucket Island garden draws inspiration
from the diminutive grid pattern of streets, cottages, and
hedged flower gardens in the town of Siasconset.

Design

The design for the garden creates a series of interconnecting
garden rooms, with vertical planes of hedge set in
juxtaposition across the horizontal plane of green lawn.
Segments of narrow brick paths lead between the privet
hedges through a series of defined spaces: an entry garden, a
perennial garden off the bedroom, a brick and fruit tree
terrace off the kitchen and living room, an herb garden, a
native shrub border, and a pergola and vine-covered brick
terrace looking out from the living room over the moor. In
the Siasconset tradition, wood trellises cover the walls and
roofs of the shingled cottage to support an abundance of
summer climbing roses.

Right top: Low, vertical planes
of privet hedge loosely define
a series of geometries across
the horizontal plane of lawn,
leading one progressively from
the diminutive scale of the
house to the larger scale of the
native landscape. **Right bottom:** Landscape site plan.
Far right: A narrow brick walk
leads from the entry garden
into the small brick and fruit
tree terrace of the house.

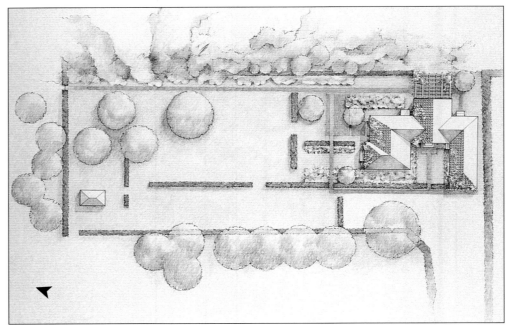

GRAND ISLE RESIDENCE

Location: Grand Isle, Vermont
Date of Completion: 1991
Owners: Withheld at client's request.
Landscape Architect: Child Associates, Inc.
Design Team: Susan F. Child (principal-in-charge), Douglas Reed, Anita Berrizbeitia
General Contractor: Distinctive Landscaping, Charlotte, VT
Photography: Child Associates, Inc.
Site Description: This eighty-acre site is located on a high peninsula on Grand Isle, overlooking Lake Champlain, VT.
Soils: Sandy, acid
USDA Plant Hardiness Zone: 4
Major Plant Materials: *Acer saccharum* (sugar maple), *Betula papyrifera* (white birch), *Fagus grandiflora* (American beech), *Fraxinus pennsylvanicus* (green ash), *Quercus rubia* (red oak), *Gaylussacia baccata* (huckleberry), *Hamamelis virginiana* (witch hazel), *Kalmia angustifolia* (sheep laurel), *Vaccinium angustifolium* (lowbush blueberry), *Vaccinium corymbosum* (highbush blueberry), *Viburnum carlesii* (fragrant viburnum).
Program: To create a unified garden with little apparent intervention into the landscape.

Design

The property comprises a beautiful natural diversity of landform and vegetation: a headland of shale cliff forested with white cedar, a slope of beech woodland, a wetland of birch and maple, a cove-edge of beach and grasses, and a high, wide meadow beyond. The groundcover throughout is fragile, diverse, and rich, consisting of blueberry, partridgeberry, and fern.

The landscape architect devised a garden scheme of the lightest touch—of the least intervention possible—to unite the diverse parts of the property into a single design. The "garden" is a system of "viewing platforms," boardwalks, steps, and pavilions which loosely join the house to the outer reaches of the property. The design's wood joinery details recall local Adirondack crafts as well as Japanese traditions of woodland retreats, in which garden structures exist in intimate relationship with nature. There is no precise definition of beginning or end to the garden's itinerary. A boardwalk floats above the fragile wetland like an island, enticing the viewer to explore the natural landscape beyond.

Right: Site sections. **Bottom right:** Landscape site plan. **Far right:** Boardwalks and stairs stretch unobtrusively through the beech forest, descending from the viewing platform at the house to the shore's edge. **Pages 44-45:** The boardwalk floats discretely, like an island above the fragile wetland—its angled segments offering shifting perspectives of the surrounding wetland, cove, and meadow.

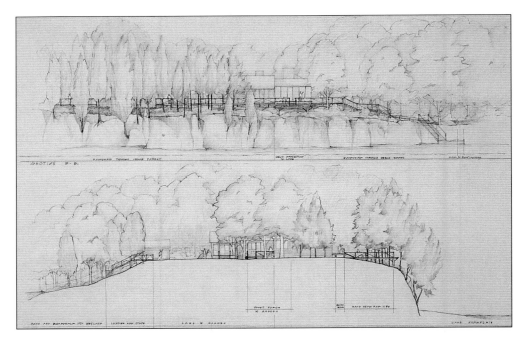

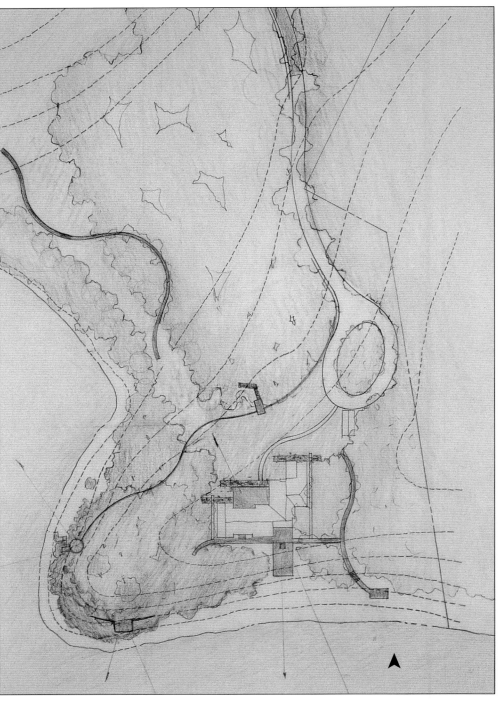

TROY RESIDENCE

Location: Troy, Ohio
Date of Completion: 1991
Owners: Withheld at client's request.
Landscape Architect: Child Associates, Inc.
Design Team: Susan F. Child (principal-in-charge),
Douglas Reed, Anita Berrizbeitia
Landscape Contractor: Siebenthaler's Nurseries,
Dayton, OH
Photography: Child Associates, Inc.
Site Description: A French provincial-style house situated
on a five-acre plateau edged by farmland, woodland, and
occasional houses.
Soils: Loam, alkaline
USDA Plant Hardiness Zone: 6
Major Plant Materials: *Aesculus glabra* (Ohio buckeye),
Aesculus hippocastanum (horsechestnut), *Crataegus crus-galli*
(cock spur hawthorn), *Crataegus viridis* 'Winter King'
(green hawthorn), *Magnolia acuminata* (cucumber tree),
Picea abies (Norway spruce), *Amelanchier canadensis* (shad),
Cornus alternifolia (pagoda dogwood), *Ligustrum amurense*
(amur privet), *Philadelphus coronarius* (mock orange),
Syringa vulgaris 'Mrs. Marshall' (lilac), *Taxus cuspidata*
(upright yew), *Viburnum dentatum* (arrowwood),
Liquidambar styraciflua (sweetgum), *Platanus* x *hybrida* var.
'Bloodgood' (London planetree), *Taxodium distichum*
(common bald cypress), *Malus* var. 'Cortland,' 'Granny
Smith,' & 'McIntosh' (apple varieties), *Betula nigra, Halesia
monticola* (mountain silverbell), *Liriodendron tulipifera*
(tulip tree), *Malus hupehensis* (tea crab), P*yrus calleryana*
'Bradford' (Bradford pear), *Tilia americana pyramidalis*
(American linden), *Cercis canadensis* (eastern redbud—
multi-stemmed), *Salix niobe* (weeping willow), *Quercus
shumardii* (Shumard oak), *Diospyros virginiana* (common
persimmon)
Major Hardscape Material: Bluestone
Program: The owners wanted the garden immediately
surrounding the house to have an abundance of flowers and
a pool.

Right: A bluestone walk and formal row of pear trees underplanted with a thick bouquet of flowers and box separate the house from the entry court on the north side. **Below right:** Landscape site plan. **Far right:** A detail of the iron gate at the entry to the garden on the north side of the house.

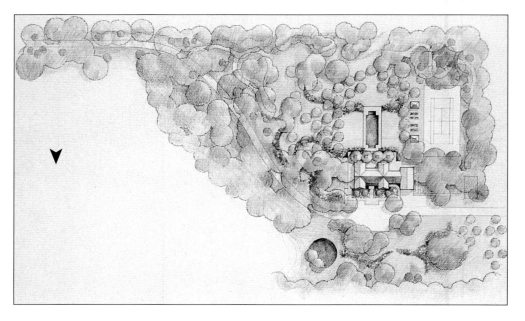

Right: On the south side, a formal row of linden trees separates the house from a long reflecting pool.

Design

Using the existing architecture as the point of departure, a formal row of flowering pear trees, underplanted with a thick bouquet of box, astilbe, peonies, roses, and lilies separates the house and the paved entry court on the north side of the house. On the south side, a large reflecting pool is set symmetrically into a bluestone terrace and is separated from the house by a formal row of linden trees.

Long ribbons of perennial flowering plants and shrubs, day lilies, and spirea weave informally from the bluestone terrace beneath an orchard to form glades of mock orange and oakleaf hydrangeas, and ravines of iris, petasites, and lysimachia, which connect in turn to the Ohio woodland and farmland at the perimeter of the property.

Although the design takes its cue from the architecture of the house, it is the horticultural components that provide the structure of the garden, leading the viewer from glade to glade in a rich succession of seasonal bloom to join the woodland and farmland beyond.

Susan Child has created many award-winning private gardens, historic landscapes, public parks, campus master plans, and site designs. Foremost among those are designs for private clients in Richmond, MA; Grand Isle, VT; Troy, OH; and Nantucket Island, MA; and the collaborative designs for South Cove Park and North Cove's Belvedere Park at Battery Park City, NY.

Topher Delaney & Andrea Cochran

CARIBBEAN CALYPSO

Location: Marin County, California
Date of Completion: 1989
Owners: Withheld at client's request.
Landscape Architect: Delaney, Cochran & Castillo, 156 South Park, San Francisco, CA 94107
Design Team: Topher Delaney, Pedro Castillo
General Contractor: Topher Delaney
Site Description: Suburban lot with screening.
USDA Plant Hardiness Zone: 9
Major Plant Materials: *Rosa banksiae, Hedera helix variegated*
Major Hardscape Materials: Stucco, concrete, metal, fabric
Program: To create a colorful, vibrant garden.

Design

A passion for the colors and forms reminiscent of the Caribbean are immediately evident as one passes through this garden bathed in peach and saffron colored light, reflections of the boundaries of tinted stucco walls surrounding the entrance to the garden. A thick blue river of concrete meanders through a grid of geometric score lines. A symbolic door is placed at the end of the garden to signify the opportunity of personal choice. Set within the core of the garden is a pool for immersion and contemplation, positioned to reflect the surrounding stands of cypress. Adjacent to the pool is a boundary of white Banksia roses spilling over a twenty-foot-high armature of metal and fabric poles, creating a layer of scented luxurious growth.

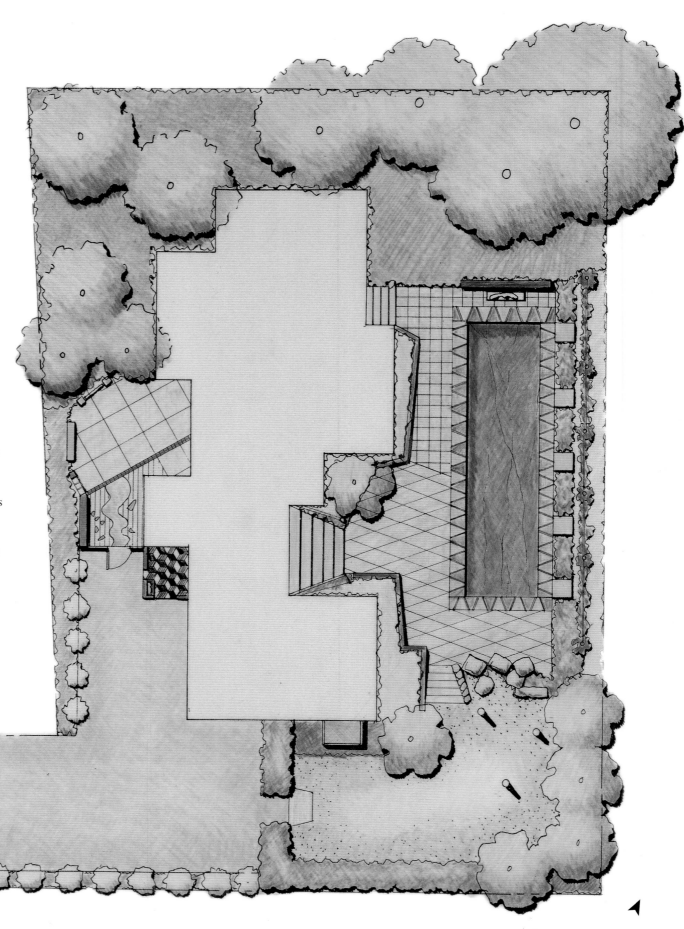

Left: Landscape site plan.
Top right: The east garden looking south: a sensuous river of dyed blue concrete with polychromed walls.
Below right: A detail of the west garden pool terrace walls with surrealistic cups.

FISH STORIES

Location: California
Date of Completion: 1996
Owners: Withheld at client's request.
Landscape Architect: Delaney, Cochran & Castillo
Design Team: Topher Delaney, Andrea Cochran, Pasqual Castillo
General Contractor: Delaney, Cochran & Castillo
Site Description: Small urban lot
Soil: Clay
USDA Plant Hardiness Zone: 9
Major Plant Materials: Queen palms, Moroblood oranges, climbing white Iceberg roses, Sago palms
Major Hardscape Materials: California crushed rocks, gold gravel, shells
Lighting: Candles, standard voltage uplights in trees and at the rear wall; all other lighting is low voltage.
Program: The client wanted a garden to view from the two stories above; a garden in which to entertain; and a garden in strong contrast to the architecture of the house.

Design

An Italian paradise of sensual pleasure consisting of a walled garden of shells, mirrors, white roses, white wisteria, and gravel courtyards. The access to the garden is direct and gracious, and can be viewed from several levels. The use of water is minimal. The walls are studded with mirrors and appear pierced, creating a slightly theatrical design. The boundaries recede into visual layers of shells and white wisteria.

Below, clockwise from top left: West wall with mussel shells and mirrors, pigmented concrete, and candles for illumination; detail of spa and shells embedded in purple stucco.

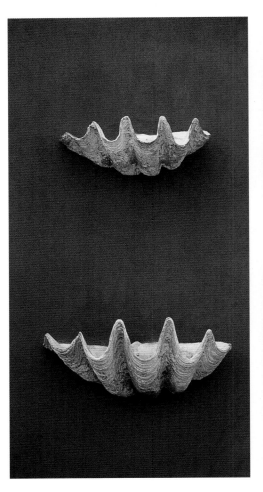 

Above: Looking south at the white concrete wall with mussel shells and spa with shells and shell wall fountain. **Right:** A presentation drawing (oil crayons) of the garden by Topher Delaney.

SITE SCULPTURE

Location: Connecticut
Date of Completion: Ongoing
Owners: Withheld at client's request.
Landscape Architect: Delaney, Cochran & Castillo
Design Team: Topher Delaney, Andrea Cochran, E.B. Min,
Morgan Hare
General Contractor: Client
Photography: Topher Delaney with drawings by E.B. Min.
Site Description: Four acres with adjoining woodlands.
Soils: Clay, loam, stone
USDA Plant Hardiness Zone: 6
Major Plant Materials: *Fagus sylvatica atropurpurea*,
boxwood, *Calamagrostis stricta, Imperata cylindrica, Sedum*
'Autumn Joy', *Sedum* 'Vera Jameson', *Nepeta* 'Six Hills
Giant'
Major Hardscape Materials: Stainless steel, paved
parquetry, stone
Program: To create a harmonious garden of many levels.

Left: Presentation drawings by E.B. Min of the bridge deck.

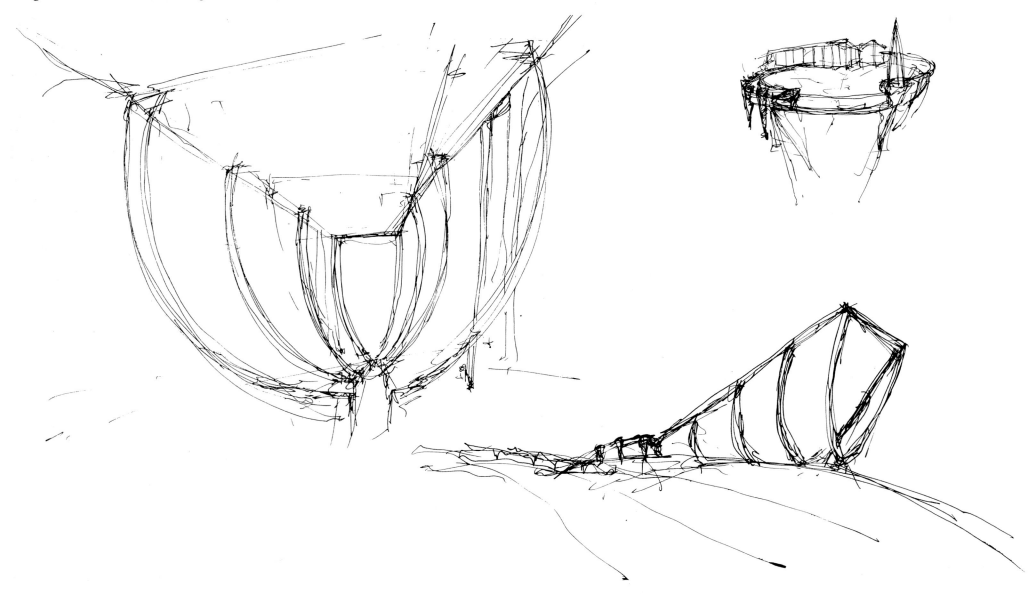

Design

A sensuous plane of white concrete bisects formal stainless steel trapezoidal walls to create the auto court. Tangents of centripetal sculptural forms compress and expand the surrounding land to create planes of an interlocking series of paved parquetry. The articulated grid of *Fagus sylvatica atropurpurea* explodes the static constructed geometry of arcing and trapezoidal vertical planes which defines the canvas of the auto court. An illusory context of harmony is effected by the boundary of the constructed stone wall.

Topher Delaney's twenty-five year career as a landscape designer, contractor, and artist encompasses a wide variety of projects including residential gardens, rooftop gardens, and sanctuary gardens for medical facilities. Andrea Cochran is a graduate of Harvard University's Graduate School of Design. She has practiced professionally since 1979. In 1989 the two landscape architects formed the firm of Delaney, Cochran & Castillo.

Chris Dunn

BILL AND CAROLYN STUTT GARDEN

Location: Stratton Mountain, Vermont
Date of Completion: 1992
Owners: Bill and Carolyn Stutt
Landscape Architect: Dunn Associates, 266 South Union Street, Burlington, VT 05401
Design Team: Chris Dunn, Ken Sellick, John Rooney
Architect: Kohn, Pederson, Fox (Bill Pederson)
General Contractor: Amorex (Peter Laffin)
Landscape Contractor: Homestead Landscape (Tom Wright)
Photography: Charles Meyer, Chris Dunn
Site Description: High elevation, steep hillside, southern exposure
Soils: Rocky, acidic soil
USDA Plant Hardiness Zone: 4B
Major Plant Materials: White spruce, white birch, lowbush blueberry, arrowwood viburnum, day lilies, bunchberry
Major Hardscape Materials: Pennsylvania bluestone, Corinthian granite, granite curb
Lighting: Lumiere 12 Volt
Building Description: A single-family mountain home designed for relaxed living and entertaining. The house is a composition of simple and complex forms built with rugged and durable materials. The landscape architecture team viewed the Stutt House as a piece of sculpture placed within the natural landscape.
Program: The client required a low-maintenance, natural landscape that integrates house with site; a perimeter path that allows one to experience house and site; and an outdoor sitting area.

Design

Development of a variety of outdoor spaces was initially explored for this project but discarded due to the rugged nature of the site and sculptural qualities of the house. During construction of the house, Dunn Associates was hired to assist with minor details. A landscape plan had not been developed. A substantial rock cut was required to access the site, resulting in an unsightly gash in the landscape. After some thought, a simple design was developed guiding all future design decisions. The site was envisioned as a mix of mountain and forest. The mountain component was to be rugged exposed rock with very little planting. The forest was to be a softer landscape of indigenous trees, understory shrubs, and ground cover of low shrubs or fescue grasses. A palette of plant materials responding to the natural conditions of the site was then developed.

Far right: View of house from the west edge of the "Alpine Meadow." **Right:** Grove of Birch trees. **Bottom:** Landscape site plan.

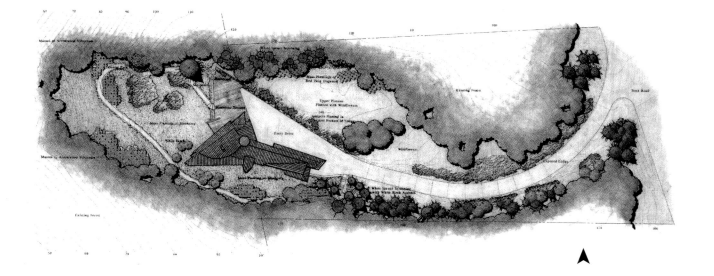

The forest side of the drive was planted with white spruce, white birch, viburnum, and fescue grass, creating a soft, naturalistic landscape, which is in sharp contrast to the mountain side of exposed ledge that is clean, sharp, and devoid of planting.

The need for a planting plan around the house became apparent as construction progressed. The owners' request for a low-maintenance landscape encouraged the design team to explore plant options that would thrive on the site. A list of two dozen alkaline soil-loving native shrubs and ground covers was prepared and researched. The landscape architects felt strongly that the palette should be limited to a mass planting of one or two plant types. Lowbush blueberry mixed with bunchberry was selected to create a pedestal surrounding the house. The western half of the site is designated the "Alpine Meadow" with lowbush blueberry interspersed among the exposed ledge. A dramatic stone stairway is woven between the ledge and down the "meadow." Stone stairs lead to a deer path along the southern side of the house. Here the palette is inspired by Beatrix Farrand's "Spirit Walk" with heather-like lowbush blueberry creating a verdant ground plane contrasted with the vertical elements of the existing white birch and arrowwood viburnum.

An outdoor terrace was developed off the dining room, punctuating the terminus of the arrival court. The 1200-square-foot bluestone terrace is organized into three connecting sections: dining area with sitting wall, open terrace, and barbecue. The terrace is a well-used space where family and friends gather while enjoying views of the alpine meadow and a framed vista of Stratton Mountain Village.

GERRY AND SANDRA GOLDBERG GARDEN

Location: Stowe, Vermont
Date of Completion: 1991
Owners: Gerry Goldberg and family
Landscape Architect: Dunn Associates
Design Team: Chris Dunn, Gail Henderson-King
Architect: Bernard Rosen, Montreal, Quebec, Canada
General Contractor: Slayton Landscape, Stowe, VT
Photography: Chris Dunn, Charles Meyer
Site Description: North-facing plateau
Soil: Rocky clay
USDA Plant Hardiness Zone: 3B
Major Plant Materials: Trees: white birch, sugar maple, littleleaf linden, apples, crabapples, Japanese tree lilac; shrubs: cotoneaster, daphne, juniper, honeysuckle, rhododendrons, roses, spirea, lowbush blueberry, viburnum; perennials: ferns, lily of the valley, trout lily, day lily, siberian iris, periwinkle, and thirty-five additional varieties of perennials.
Major Hardscape Materials: Pennsylvania bluestone, locally quarried stone, granite curbing, gravel drive
Lighting: BK Lighting (12-volt)
Building Description: A new single-family residence designed as a weekend retreat for a professional couple and their grown children. The condensed massing of the exterior reflects the northern Vermont farmyard vernacular. Interior and exterior spaces were generously sized to accommodate daily family living as well as large events.
Program: The program required a large entry court, small service court with garage, formal living room lawn and garden, perennial gardens, hot tub garden, pool area, walking trails, campfire overlook, tennis court, and golf practice range (two greens with three tee boxes).

Design

Organized into a sequence of seven gardens, the landscape responds to circulation needs and is an extension of the interior rooms. Reflecting the design of the house, the character of the gardens varies depending on whether they are associated with the public, semi-public, or private zones of the residence. The entry courtyard and garden provide a welcoming and elegant arrival point. Defined along one side by a stone wall that steps up and integrates with the garage, a visitor is directed to the elevated, recessed front door by a forced perspective composed of the wall, low stone walls, and compressed steps.

A simple palette of juniper, Japanese tree lilac, and Little Princess spirea complement the geometry of the house at the front door. Passing through the transitional garden one can choose to walk down into the secret garden, filled with

Right: An aerial view of the garden looking east. **Below:** Landscape site plan. **Far right:** View from the pool into the formal lawn.

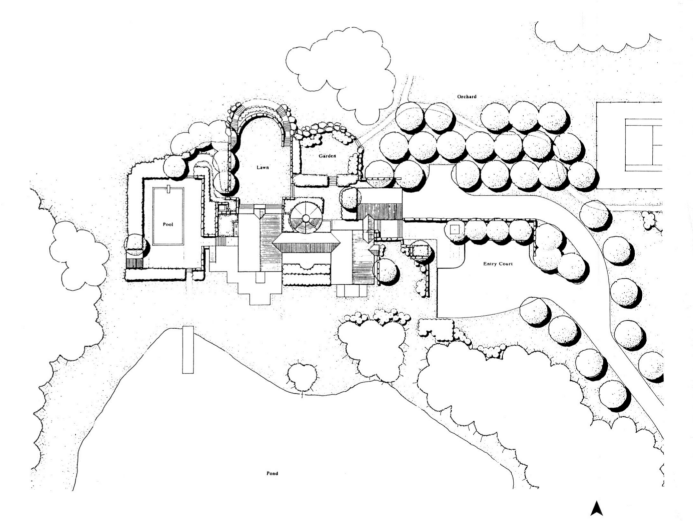

Below right: Garden path to
pool and pond. **Bottom left:**
Entry courtyard. **Bottom center:** Entry progression.
Bottom right: Formal lawn
and perennial garden.

perennials and enclosed with a mix of boulder and stone
walks, or step into the formal lawn, which is a long
rectangle with circular terminus overlooking the lower
meadows and mountains beyond. The lawn is an extension
of the house's great room and is defined by a slight grade
change and stone and boulder walls. Juxtaposed against the
formality of the space and materials are large boulders and a
mix of perennials.

A naturalistic garden of white birch, lowbush blueberry, and
cotoneaster separates the formal lawn and pool area. The
pool is located mid-level between the main and lower level of
the house providing easy access from the game and changing
rooms on the lower level and the main living space of the
first floor and matches the surrounding natural grade.

An extensive deck off the kitchen and dining room posed a
landscape challenge for the area below. A hot tub room
located on the lower level looked out underneath the deck
to the pond. Fortuitously, the architect had utilized massive
12 x 12 foot posts for the deck's support. These were
visualized as tree trunks and the shady, sloped ground as a
dark forest floor. Large boulders interspersed with woodland
perennials and highlighted with night lighting were placed
to create an attractive composition from any vantage point.

A tennis court with an out building was located on axis
with the entry walkway. A pair of challenging golf greens
with sand traps and pond, and three different tee boxes,
were designed to provide the owner and guests with a wide
variety of practice opportunities.

STONE HILL FARM GARDENS

Location: Vermont
Date of Completion: 1991
Owners: Withheld at client's request.
Landscape Architect: Dunn Associates
Design Team: Chris Dunn, Gail Henderson-King, Tom Conrey
Architects: Alan Wanzenberg, Scott Cornelius
Contractors: Ted Curto (stone mason), Mosher Excavation (earthwork), Shepard Butler (landscape contractor), Custom Pool of New England
Photography: Charles Meyer
Site Description: Steep, south-facing hillside
Soil: Sandy
USDA Plant Hardiness Zone: 3B
Major Plant Materials: Trees: white birch, sugar maple, yellowwood, white spruce, and white pines; shrubs: hydrangea, Bar Harbor, and Andorra juniper, mugho pine, spirea, high bush blueberry; perennials: twenty-eight varieties.
Major Hardscape Materials: Pennsylvania bluestone, locally collected boulders, Corinthian granite, local fieldstone, chip-seal asphalt drive
Lighting: B.K. Lighting (12-volt)
Building Description: A new single-family home designed for extensive entertaining and as a comfortable year-round residence. The house was designed to blend with the natural environment and to evoke the National Park Service architecture of the 1920s and 1930s.
Program: The clients wanted the design team to create separate arrival and service courts; a formal terrace off the living room; an informal terrace off kitchen overlooking the pool; a landscape separation between library and access drive.

Design

A seven-acre meadow edge site was selected for its solar orientation, magnificent views, and sense of enclosure provided by mature pines, oaks, maples, and birch. Siting of the house was a joint effort by the clients, architect, and landscape architect. The position and elevation were carefully considered to ensure proper fit of the house into the hillside, with the right proportions of cut in the courtyards and fill in front of the terraces. The completed project balanced cut and fills as well as provided a panoramic view of mountains and valleys with intimate views into surrounding ravines and hillsides.

The landscape design evolved from the rugged character of the site and responds to the progression of the house. The northern side offers intimate, enclosed spaces that welcome one to the house and provide detailed views of the architecture, shade garden, and surrounding hillside meadows. The south side contrasts the entry zone with broad expansive views and landscape elements that are in keeping with this scale.

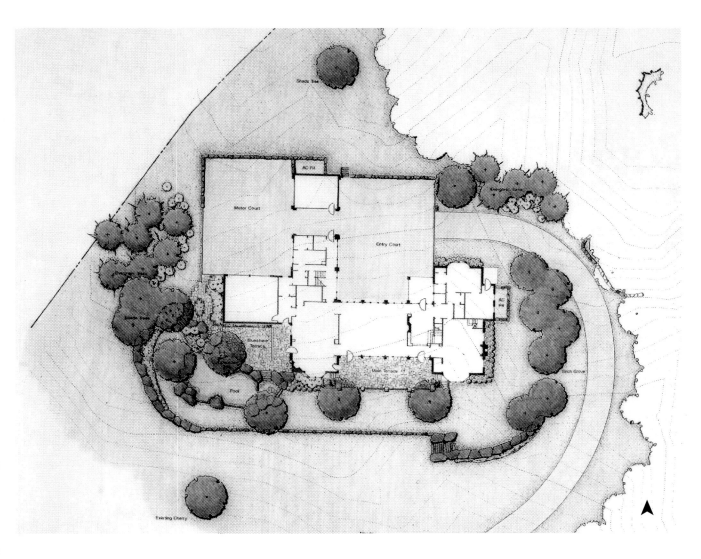

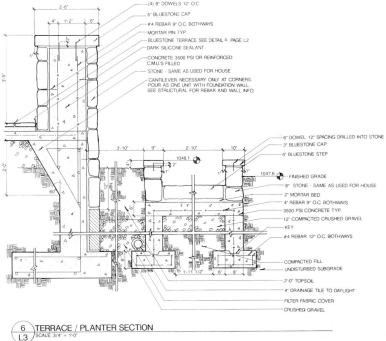

TERRACE / PLANTER SECTION
SCALE: 3/4" = 1'-0"

The property consists of five distinct gardens. The north slope is a natural meadow ringed with mature white pines and maple trees. The native fescue grasses have been maintained, and provide a wonderful progression of texture and color throughout the seasons. The arrival court has a small shade garden that relies on a variety of textures to complement the romantic nature of the architecture.

A woodland garden separating the library and drive was created using mature paper birch trees, ferns, European ginger, lily of the valley, and vinca minor. A mass of junipers creates a threshold and transition with the main terrace lawn area. This expansive space utilizes simple symmetry and plant selection to provide the user with a sense of enclosure while framing views of the adjacent meadows, valleys, and distant mountains.

The pool garden was envisioned as a glacial pool surrounded by exposed ledge. A series of massive boulder walls characteristic of surrounding natural ledge were constructed to form two level areas for the pool and the terrace. The architects had a strong vision for the character of the stonework and the transition between more formal dry stack walls and the rustic boulder walls. The planting of shrubs and perennials helped with the transition from formal terrace to the informal, naturalistic garden around the pool. Bluestone paving mixed with natural stone coping around the pool and boulders combine with an informal mix of trees, shrubs, and perennials to create an attractive, relaxed environment.

PRIVATE GARDEN

Right: Garden looking west.
Below left: Garden edge.
Below right: Perspective sketch looking west.

Location: Northeastern United States
Date of Completion: 1990
Owners: Withheld at client's request.
Landscape Architect: Dunn Associates with The Office of Dan Kiley
Design Team: Chris Dunn, Julie Compoli, Gail Henderson-King, Dan Kiley
General Contractor: Al Ulmer and Terry Dinnan
Photography: Chris Dunn
Site Description: Cut into the hillside, the terrace is located on the south side of the house overlooking a pond and distant lake.
Soil: Heavy clay
USDA Plant Hardiness Zone: 4
Major Plant Materials: Horse chestnut, serviceberry, vinca, perennials, existing apple trees
Major Hardscape Materials: Locally quarried stone
Building Description: A 150-year-old farmhouse used by a large family for weekend retreats and to oversee their farm operations. Ten years earlier the previous owners had partially restored the house.
Program: The landscape architect was asked to design an outdoor terrace for family gatherings and meals in keeping with the house and surrounding landscape, and to provide a sun pocket that was out of the wind but took advantage of cooling summer breezes.

Design

The terrace was seen as a landscape element creating a smooth transition between the house and the surrounding agricultural fields. The design components were initially reduced to their most basic function of floor, walls, and ceiling. Once the basics were defined, specific plant materials and precise detailing of hardscape elements provided visual interest and a simple elegance.

Located on the south side of the house, off the kitchen-area dining room, the site provided wonderful views of the lake and mountains. Numerous options were studied prior to developing a balanced composition of positive and negative space unifying house and landscape.

The main terrace is surrounded on three sides by a twenty-inch-high seating wall. Against the house, the wall covers an unattractive exposed foundation, while the top of the west wall is flush with the surrounding land, creating a visual datum line connecting the house, terrace, and surrounding mountains into a single composition. The terrace was designed to be a paved, hardscape space. Where plants were needed, they were set into planting beds cut out of the stone paving. A bosque of single stem serviceberry (*Amelanchier canadensis*) and ground cover of periwinkle

Below: Detail of terrace wall.
Right: Garden stair.
Far right: Landscape site
plan.

(*Vinca minor*) forms the diaphanous edge to this space and creates a portal into the softer shade garden.

The shade garden, twelve inches below the terrace, consists of a lawn floor and is defined by a continuation of the main terrace low stone wall with existing crabapple and mulberry trees incorporated into the plan. Perennial flowers provide seasonal interest and further soften the space, partially screening the stone wall edge. Hardscape materials in the shade garden are surrounded by plant material.

Chris Dunn is a landscape architect who grew up and continues to live in Burlington, Vermont. His early interest in landscape architecture and garden design was cultivated by grandparents who had developed extensive landscaped gardens at their home in Essex, Connecticut. Work as a landscape contractor through high school and college instilled in him an appreciation for native plant material and their environmental requirements. He was educated at Cornell University and spent five years as an associate of noted landscape architect Dan Kiley. Chris then formed his own firm, Dunn Associates which was awarded a Progressive Architecture Citation for Planning in 1987 and the firm's work has been featured in several design magazines.

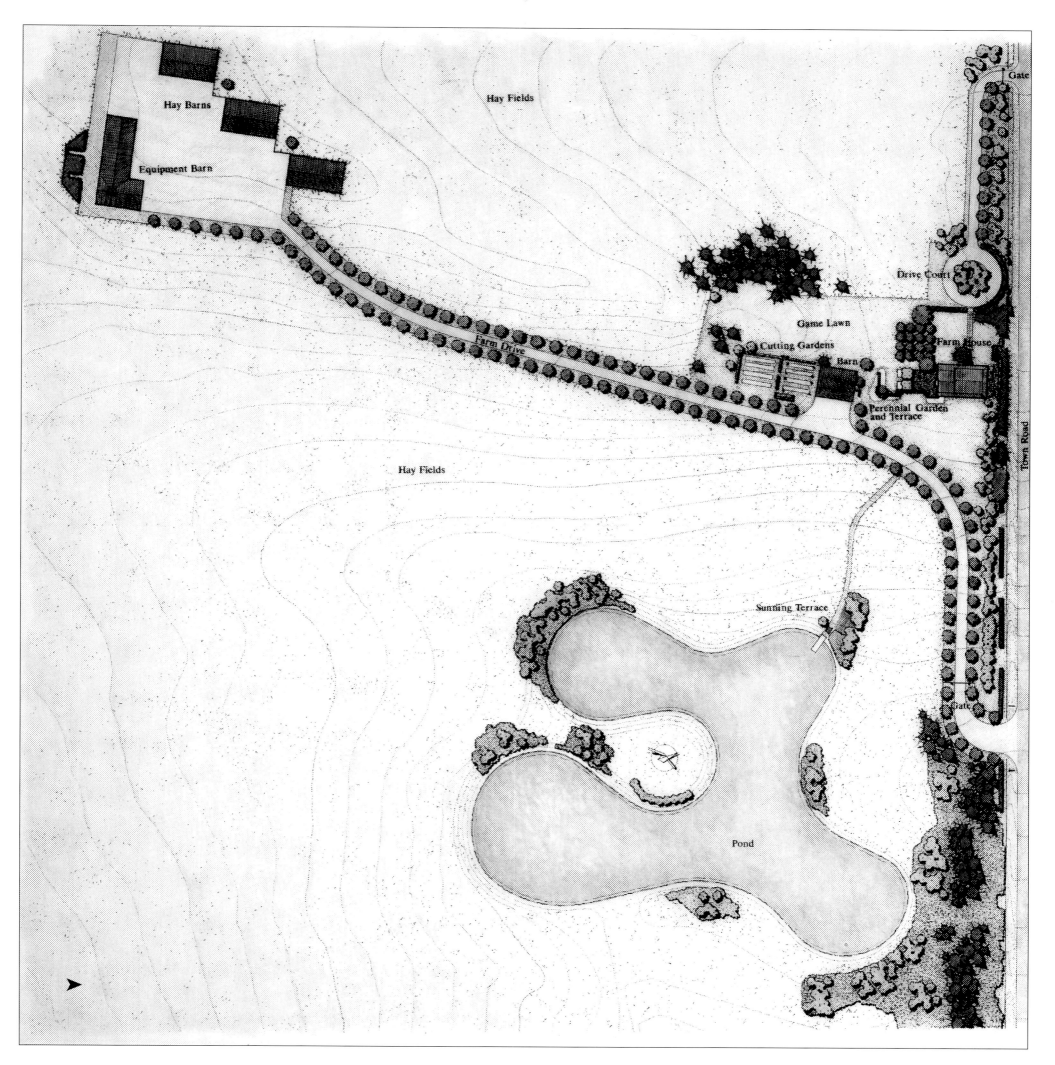

Hay Fields

Hay Barns

Equipment Barn

Gate

Drive Court

Game Lawn

Cutting Gardens

Barn

Farm House

Farm Drive

Perennial Garden and Terrace

Hay Fields

Town Road

Sunning Terrace

Gate

Pond

Isabelle C. Greene

TERRACED HILLSIDE GARDEN

Location: Montecito, California
Date of Completion: 1985
Owners: Withheld at client's request.
Landscape Architect: Isabelle C. Greene & Associates, 1236 Chipala Street, Suite 200, Santa Barbara, CA 93101
Architect: Warren & Gray Inc.
Contractors: Chole Morgan (planting, irrigation, and soil); Kenneth Urton (fabrication of terrace walls); Michael Schmidt (artist and metal sculptor for fabrication of copper arbor and copper light fixtures), Oswald Da Ros (stonework), Pat Scott Masonry (stonework)
Photography: Isabelle C. Greene
Lighting: Frank Burnaby & Associates
Site Description: Awkwardly steep hillside within a natural oak woodland
Soil: Gumbo clay with poor drainage
USDA Plant Hardiness Zone: 10
Major Plant Materials: Native succulents, Mediterranean-type plants, nonthirsty shrubs and groundcovers, roses, edible fruits, herbs, and vegetables.
Major Hardscape Materials: Sandstone boulders, slate, gravel, decomposed granite, formed concrete walls, and stucco/CMU walls
Building Description: Modern pueblo-style structure
Program: The site had severe water restrictions and therefore design decisions were made accordingly. The client wanted a Zen garden as well as edible and flowering plants.

Right: Mulberry trees weep over the garden like green fountains.

Design

Although a Zen garden was requested, the landscape architect chose to furnish it with beige gravel and southwestern plants, respecting the southwest architecture of the house. "I feel a need to carry its design back into the landscape," she said. The client had a large family property in the Sierra Nevada Mountains which contained a pristine spring. The landscape architect was asked to recreate that spring for this garden. This is the only significant use of water in the plan and creates something of an oasis effect as one enters or leaves through the front door where the spring is located.

Far left: Sections of planting resemble farm fields as viewed from high above. **Above:** Mud-like walls were made of colored concrete poured into formwork of cedar shakes.

GENTLE VALLEY WATERCOURSE

Location: Santa Ynez, California
Date of Completion: 1982
Owners: Withheld at client's request.
Landscape Architect: Isabelle C. Greene
Landscape Contractor: Ron Foil Landscapes (planting and irrigation); Cliff Solem (house and landscape structures contractor); Pat Scott Masonry and Cal Real Pool (boulders and pool/spa); Peter Crane (Astrostone contractor)
Photography: Isabelle C. Greene
Lighting: Frank Burnaby & Associates
Site Description: Gentle grassy valley on a ranch with oaks.
Soil: Extremely porous
USDA Plant Hardiness Zone: 10.
Major Plant Materials: Native shrubs and groundcovers, informal grasses, flowering beds, native annual wildflowers
Major Hardscape Materials: Adobe walls, Saltillo tile pavers, Astrostone-surfaced concrete
Building Description: Small, older ranch-like house of adobe block with tile roof; the interior has been completely remodeled.
Program: The landscape architect was asked to create a recreational garden for three separate families who own a business together in Los Angeles and use this property for a weekend getaway. The program included integrating a swimming pool, large spa, tennis court, barbecue, car park, and terrace into a cohesive design. The challenge for the landscape architect was to fit all of these requirements beautifully and believably into the wild quality of the property.

Design

A key to the design is the swimming pool which appears gently slung into the valley, rather than cutting a hard line across it. The landscape architect designed a sloping "sandy beach" visually at one side of the pool while the other side gently climbs up a sloping rock embankment. The "beach" is actually an apron of concrete, surfaced with fine sand particles held in polymer. Larger pebbles and some stones are strewn through to better resemble a natural shore. Birds and kids are able to walk down the beach and wade into the pool.

The tennis court is placed far enough up-valley so as to be obscured in the oak woodland, and the patio is designed in such a way that it appears to flow from the house.

Below: Flowers and rocks converse at pool's edge.
Bottom: The unusual shape of this pool adds to its natural charm.

Above: The ranch's rear land-scape gives way to the Santa Ynez hills beyond. **Right:** The pool's "sandy beach" invites wading by all ages and by critters as well.

COLORFUL SEASIDE COLLABORATION

Location: Carpinteria, California
Date of Completion: 1995
Owners: Withheld at client's request.
Landscape Architect: Isabelle C. Greene
Design Team: Isabelle Greene, Paul Tuttle
Architect: Robert Garland
Contractors: Turk Hessellund Nursery, Ray Sodomka, Don and Dave Harris (plantings); Carl Hill (irrigation)
Photography: Isabelle C. Greene
Lighting: Frank Burnaby & Associates
Site Description: A wooded cliff edge overlooking the ocean, flanked by lush ravines
Soil: Loamy
USDA Plant Hardiness Zone: 10
Major Plant Materials: Native shrubs and groundcovers; color supplied by bougainvillea, verbena, dianthus, felicia, agapanthus
Major Hardscape Materials: Concrete aggregate paving; other "paved" surfaces of round stones evocative of the beach or a riverbed, set in sand; free-standing stucco walls.
Building Description: Modern clean-lined wood volumes with concrete aggregate chimney and splash block. The entry and front door were obscure and confusing.
Program: The client desired a collaborative solution to the existing building entry problem by bringing together the landscape architect and the designer, Paul Tuttle. The result was a bold and cohesive design for the architecture and the garden. Tuttle designed the curved walls (each of a different height and color), front gate, and handrails, to sweep visitors towards the hidden front door. All three (designer, client, and landscape architect) collaborated on the colors and arrangement of the glazed pots.

Design

Both the garden and hardscape combine earth tones with bright, brilliant primaries. Fire engine reds are sparked back and forth between handrails and bougainvillea, muted blues play along the several heights of agapanthus umbels and the bright blue senecio ground cover, finishing out through felicia and plumbago. Earth-toned gazanias stretch in between, while singular stands of anigozanthos in museum-like solitude seem to reflect both sides of the moon-shaped window.

The result is a spare, clean, modern design with clear definition between plant masses and nonplant areas. All of the plants are drought-tolerant.

Right: The kangaroo paws, the walls, and even the handrails are carefully placed as sculpture in this garden.

During her twenty-five years of practice, Isabelle C. Green has created over four hundred gardens which bear her mark of effortless design coupled with extensive use of natural forms. After receiving a bachelor's degree in botany from UCLA in 1956, she completed post-graduate work in studio arts at UCSB and in landscape architecture at the University of Oregon and UCLA. (Photo by Diane Foster)

Far left: Colorful walls generate a bold and simple garden design. **Above:** The circular window frames the garden beyond.

Richard Haag

SOMMERVILLE GARDEN

Location: Lake Washington, Medina, Washington
Date of Completion: 1990
Owners: Mimi and Slim Sommerville
Landscape Architect: Richard Haag Associates, Inc., 2335 Eastlake Avenue West, Seattle, WA 98102
Design Team: Richard Haag, FASLA (lead designer)
Architect: Robert Small, FAIA, Bellevue, WA
General Contractor: Tom Paulsen Construction Co., Bellevue, WA
Consultants: Chuck Greening (artist for stream bed), Tom Small (artist for fountain orifice)
Photography: Richard Haag
Site Description: Three-quarter acre site on a narrow shelf of land that surrounds Lake Washington
USDA Plant Hardiness Zone: 6
Major Plant Materials: Bird-attracting plants including serviceberry (amelanchier), commercial blueberries, dogwoods (cornus) as shrubs, trees, and ground plants, viburnums, strawberries, privet, daphne, and winterberry (ilex); seasonal/color and special interest trees and shrubs including stewartia, common and Japanese tree lilac, katsura, serviceberry, Asian dogwood, and silverbell; multi-colored potted flowers; water-loving plants including Island of Canadian serviceberry, underplanted with stoloniferous serviceberry, sedges, rushes, iris, and lilies; deciduous and evergreen vines of clematis, wisteria, honeysuckle, and ivy; trimmed taxus hedge; liriope within the interstices of concrete wall cribbing; fern and black stem bamboo; ground covers—pachysandra, Irish moss, wooly thyme, scouring rush.
Major Hardscape Materials: Red brick pavement entry, plum-colored brick are angled to provide treadways for tires while the median band is flat for walking while angled brick curbs protect the driveway planting; retaining wall of concrete cribbing; native boulder surrounded by transported moss-covered glacial stones; fountain and stream bed with river rock; natural pool; hot tub; putting green.
Program: To connect the floor elevation of thirty feet with the street elevation of sixty-five feet with minimum impact on the site

Below: The source fountain in a granite bowl. **Bottom:** Landscape site plan. **Right:** Stony brook and pool below the main garden terrace.

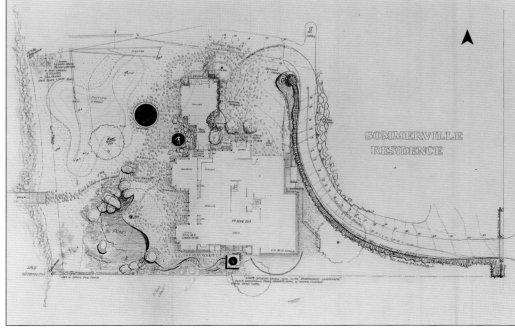

Design

A combined walkway/driveway, tightly switchbacked down the face of the bluff; outdoor terrace for garden parties as well as small areas for intimate sunset watching; running water and a pond. The client was particularly interested in a garden that changes with the seasons.

Garden stream and pool water are recirculated and any overflow from the winter rains finds its way into Lake Washington.

Above: Living wall of liriope supports taxus hedge that screens the driveway. **Right:** A bench from the garden terrace overlooks the pools.

KUKES GARDEN

Below: Wooden gate designed by the architect. **Bottom:** Stone cairn anchors the terrace and turns the steps. **Right:** Concrete paver steps lead to concrete pads.

Location: Lake Whatcom, Bellingham, Washington
Date of Completion: 1990
Owners: Wilbur and Linda Kukes
Landscape Architect: Richard Haag Associates, Inc.
Design Team: Richard Haag, FASLA (lead designer)
Architect: David Hall, Partner, The Henry Klein Partnership, Mount Vernon, WA
General Contractor: Garritt Dykstra (builder), Roger Hill (landscape contractor)
Consultants: Terry Wean, Tim Wean (stonemasons)
Photography: Richard Haag
Site Description: The site is a picturesque promontory with multiple ecotypes: mature evergreen forest, spring-fed bog, sandstone escarpment, and lake-edge swamp. An existing summer cabin was sacrificed and the new residence was sensitively sited into the tree line, thus saving the best part of the site for the terraces.
USDA Plant Hardiness Zone: 5
Major Plant Materials: Native plantings with thyme planted in grass-crete blocks.
Major Hardscape Materials: Dry stack river rock stones are mounded in undulating walls to tie the house to its environment. Patios made of river rock deposits combined with exposed aggregate concrete and brick extend off the back of the house looking over the lake. Grass-crete, cast concrete gridded blocks, are used as pavers and cut into the sandstone bank to provide stepped pathways down to the lake. The interstices of the blocks are planted with thyme and grass. A series of varyingly sized concrete pads of brushed aggregate finish "float" on the water, enabling one to venture out onto the lake. A cedar deck links the children's wing and the main wing to the outdoors.
Building Description: A large new home designed to capture the rustic character of a summer cabin or a lodge. It uses details from the Bungalow and Craftsman styles including tapered pillars, projecting beams, exposed rafters, a small gable roof, and a main entry with a small roofline to create a sheltered vestibule. The exterior is red cedar shingles. The many windows provide generous access to light and views.
Program: The program was a diverse and ambitious list of activities for both inside and outside the house, from private family activities to large social and recreational celebrations.

Design

The landscape architect worked closely with the client to preserve the forest, the mature evergreens that embrace the residence, and to heal the areas that had been damaged in the building process. The preferred plant palette was carefully incorporated into each zone. The landscape architect was responsible for site planning, landscape concept and design, planting plan, construction documents, and construction observation.

SAN JUAN
ISLAND GARDEN

Location: San Juan Island, Washington
Date of Completion: 1992
Owners: Withheld at the client's request.
Landscape Architect: Richard Haag Associates, Inc.
Design Team: Richard Haag, FASLA (lead designer)
Architect: Finholm & Finholm Architects, Aspen, CO
General Contractor: Cliff Lowe (builder/contractor).
Consultants: Island Gardens (landscape contractors),
Merle's Masonry (stone masonry), Peter Busby (sculpture)
Photography: Richard Haag
Site Description: The estate, perched above the shores of
the Strait of Juan de Fuca, is a cluster of separate specialized
structures sited among the rock, earth forms, and trees to
ensure the full range of landscape experience
USDA Plant Hardiness Zone: 5

Below: A cedar-pole deer
fence. **Bottom:** Landscape
site plan. **Right top:** The
morning court. **Right bottom:**
Earth forms establish the
morning court.

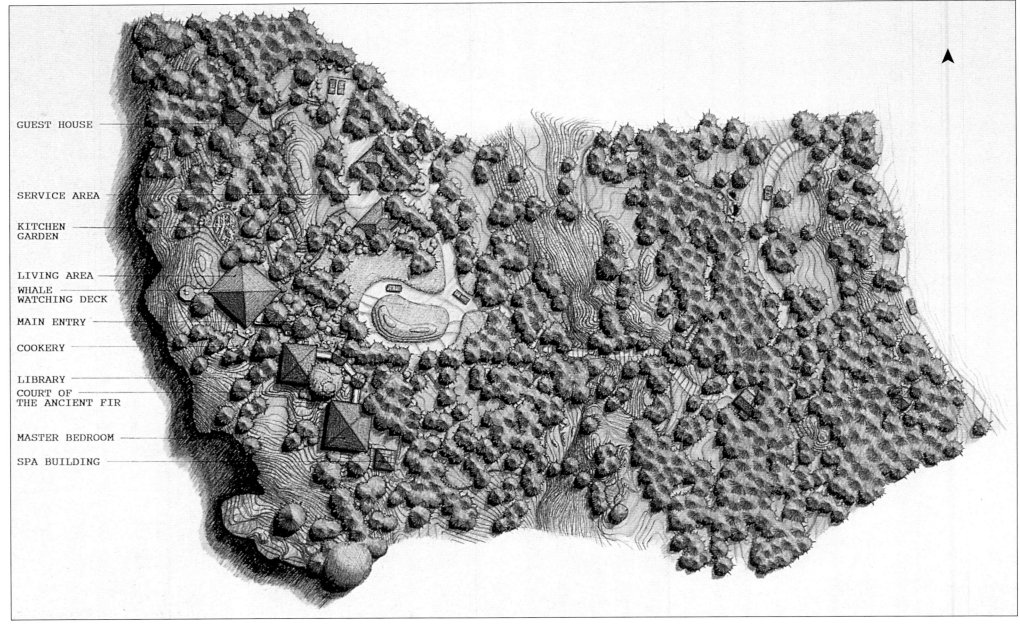

GUEST HOUSE

SERVICE AREA

KITCHEN
GARDEN

LIVING AREA
WHALE
WATCHING DECK

MAIN ENTRY

COOKERY

LIBRARY
COURT OF
THE ANCIENT FIR

MASTER BEDROOM

SPA BUILDING

Major Plant Materials: Extensive special collection of over one hundred rhododendrons and azaleas selected by the landscape architect; amelanchier *(Canadensis)*, sarcococca, camellia (*Japonicand sasanqua*), stewartia, bamboo, Asian dogwoods, *Cercidiphyllum magnificum*, gooseberry, huckleberry and blueberry, ilex, *Viburnum* sp., clethra, ferns, honeysuckle, star jasmine, lily of the valley, helleborus, iris, hostas, peonies; large collections of succulents and shade-loving plants; ground covers including *Epimedium* sp., pachysandra, *Vinca minor alba*, and various species of mosses.

Major Hardscape Materials: Flagstone entry and patio, barbecue/cookery, whale-watching deck, deer fence, and cedar pole fence

Building Description: Beauty and serenity are found in the simplicity and functionality of the structures. The home is a sequence of small, individual buildings woven through the forest and connected by an outdoor, partially covered walkway. The guest house, living area, library, and master bedroom are sequestered among the trees and gardens.

Program: The landscape architect was brought into this project early by the client and architect and was involved with all phases of site development, master planning, planting design, irrigation, lighting systems and design, the selection and placement of outdoor furniture, and the personal selection of the plants.

Design

The estate, perched above the shores of the Strait of Juan de Fuca, is a cluster of separate specialized structures sited among the exposed bedrock, earth forms, and trees to cover the full range of landscape experience. The sound and fury of the sea against the headlands is connected to the quietness of the mossy woods by a sequence of stairways and trenchworks carved into the living stone. The front entrance is hospitable and generous, like the client. There are secret gardens, "The Court of the Ancient Fir," a kitchen garden, and social spaces for entertaining throughout the site.

Richard Haag, FASLA, practices and teaches landscape architecture. He established his firm, Richard Haag Associates, thirty-seven years ago and is the lead designer on all the firm's work. Mr. Haag's skills in collaborative design, innovative thinking, community involvement, and project management are expressed in the more than 500 past built projects and current work. Internationally recognized for his creativity, sensitivity to the natural environment, and adaptive reuse of existing structures and facilities, he is the only person to twice receive the ASLA President's Award for Design Excellence.

Ron Herman

ELLISON RESIDENCE

Location: San Francisco, California
Date of Completion: 1996
Owner: Lawrence Ellison
Landscape Architect: Ron Herman, 261 Joaquin Avenue, San Leandro, CA 94577
Design Team: Ron Herman (principal designer)
Architect: Olle Lundberg, San Francisco, CA
General Contractor: Ryan Associates, San Francisco, CA; John Nishizawa Co., Martinez, CA (landscape contractor).
Photography: Mark Schwartz, San Rafael, CA
Site Description: Interior courtyard
USDA Plant Hardiness Zone: 10
Major Plant Materials: Bamboo, dwarf mondo grass, baby tears ground cover
Major Hardscape Materials: Mankato Kosata limestone
Building Description: A 10,000-square-foot house designed by architect William Wurster in 1961. The house contained twelve-foot-high ceilings with rooms that look out over the San Francisco Bay as well as inward over a central courtyard. Architect Olle Lundberg has remodeled the house creating walls of glass and stainless steel.
Program: To create a modern courtyard that would be integral to the elegant interiors and glass wall detailing. The courtyard is a central inward focus for the house and is viewed from several levels and various locations within the house. The main progression from entry to living space is alongside the garden via a glass gallery. Not unlike a Japanese temple, the garden is to be used for both viewing and as a place of contemplation.

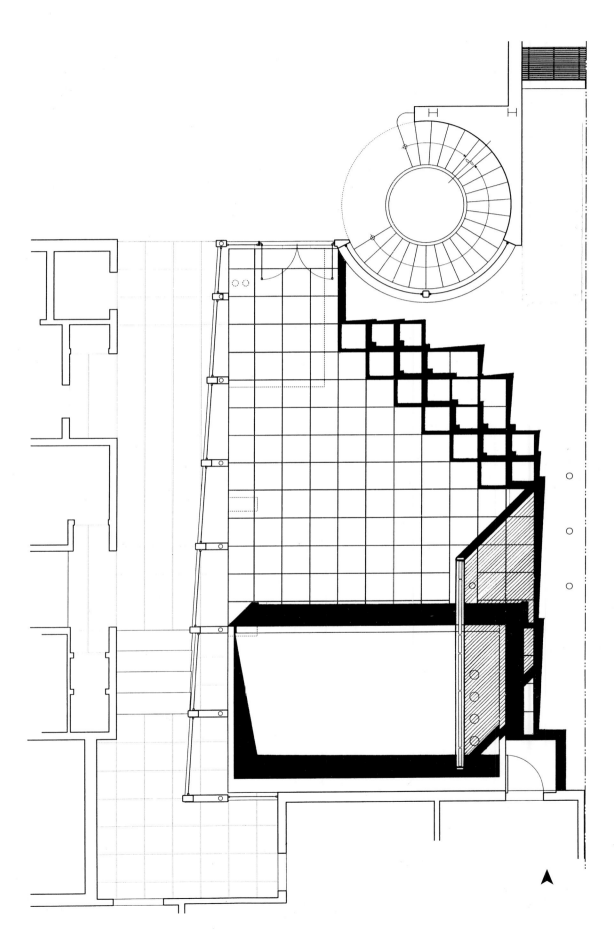

Above left: Black riverwash stones and baby tears moss. **Above right:** Detail of moss, stones, limestone pavers, and bronze grid. **Left:** Section elevation through the courtyard. **Right:** Bronze grid of moss and stones.

ELEVATION-COURT.

ELLISON RESIDENCE
SAN FRANCISCO, CA.

Design

The garden provides a strong focus for the entry, circulation, and living spaces of the house. The inspiration for the garden is a checkerboard garden of moss and stone in a Zen temple in Kyoto, Japan. This garden is a minimalist reference to that garden and was designed for a client who greatly admires Japanese traditional gardens.

A bronze metal grid is employed to achieve precision of line. The grid becomes three-dimensional with changes in elevation. A glass wall intersects a pond to mask a door in a pure white wall. Water flows over the bronze-edged pool.

Three plant materials are used in the garden: moss, mondo grass, and bamboo. The bamboo, while providing foliage, is also desirable for its sculptural qualities against a large bare wall of the adjoining residence.

The multiplicity of reflective surfaces gives an ethereal quality to the garden. Crispness of line and detail are used to give the garden a sense of elegance.

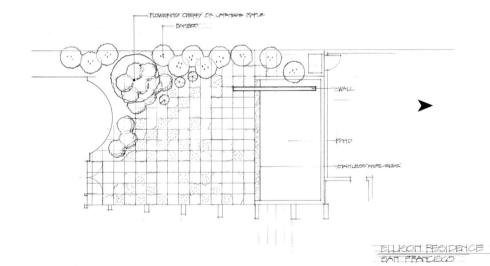

HATCH GARDEN

Location: Occidental, California
Date of Completion: 1996
Owner: Ann Hatch
Landscape Architect: Ron Herman
Design Team: Ron Herman (principal designer)
Architect: Paul Discoe, Oakland, CA
General Contractor: Joinery Structures, Oakland, CA
Consultants: Tom Ruth (furniture), Denny Abrams (floor plan)
Photography: Mark Schwartz, San Rafael, CA
Site Description: Approximately twenty acres of gently rolling landscape planted with Gravenstein apple trees.
USDA Plant Hardiness Zone: 9
Major Plant Materials: Gravenstein apple trees, flowering cherry trees, roses, *Cerastium tomentosum, Ajuga repens,* jasmine
Major Hardscape Materials: Top-stained concrete squares (poured in place)
Building Description: A country retreat consisting of two structures: a two-story residence and a guest house/cabana. The buildings are a hybrid of Japanese and rural California design that are distinguished by the fine Japanese wood joinery used throughout.
Program: This getaway residence is situated among approximately twenty acres of Gravenstein Apple trees near Occidental, CA. The working orchard is situated in the midst of a natural landscape. The climate can be quite hot in the summer, making a swimming pool a welcome addition to the site.

Design

The house and garden are laid out on a strict 3 x 3 foot grid. The orchard also has its own grided layout. The structured, homogeneous formality of the grid draws attention to those elements that are played against it in a seemingly random manner. Many elements, even plants, are made to conform to the grid and others deflect or interrupt its formality.

Like the structures, the garden seeks to combine the best elements of Japanese and California design such as the ambiguous transition between inside and outside and the "outdoor rooms" that have become associated with "California Living." The rock placement recalls both a Japanese garden and the natural rock outcroppings of local region.

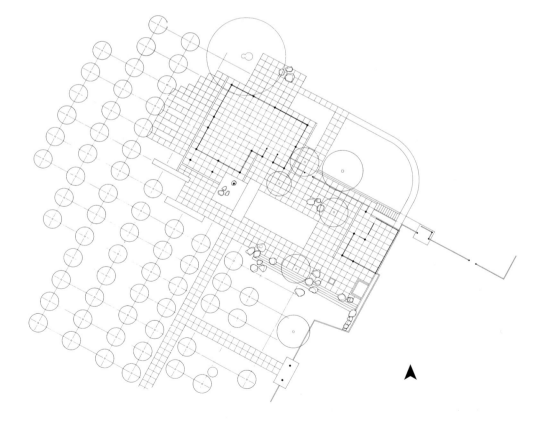

The swimming pool is placed close to the house and used as a reflecting device, and additionally forces entry over the water via a bridge. The strict grid begins to break down as it moves into the orchard landscape. The planting also becomes less confined and formal away from the house and acts as a transition to the distant plantings.

Ron Herman is a landscape architect practicing primarily in California. He specializes in residential and estate gardens. Herman was a visiting lecture for twenty years in the landscape architecture and architecture departments at the University of California, Berkeley. He lectures widely and is co-author of "A Guide to the Gardens of Kyoto."

Top: View of garden looking towards the main house. **Left:** Early site study. **Right:** Grid with plantings (cerastium and ajuga).

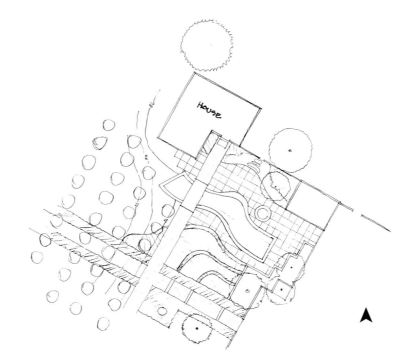

Raymond Jungles

GOLDEN BEACH GARDEN

Location: Golden Beach, Florida
Date of Completion: 1995
Owners: Nicholas and Catalina Landes
Landscape Architect: Raymond Jungles, Inc., P.O. Box 1762, Coconut Grove, FL 33233
Architect: Carlos Zapata
General Contractor: Cruz Rodrigez General Contractors
Landscape Contractor: Plant Creations, Inc.
Consultants: Bobby Altman (architectural consultant)
Lighting: Combination low-voltage and line voltage
Photography: Raymond Jungles
Site Description: Beachfront lot
Soils: Sand and fill with some imported planting soil
USDA Plant Hardiness Zone: 10
Major Plant Materials: Native species, bamboo, palms, cycads
Major Hardscape Materials: Concrete, keystone, granite.
Building Description: The residence was built on the footprint of an existing Mediterranean residence. The architect, Carlos Zapata, along with Catalina designed a sculptural, airy, dramatic structure.
Program: The program consisted of three major requirements: to design a garden which complemented the unique design of the residence—the garden had to be bold yet soft, appear natural or "thrown" as the client said; to contain all off-site views towards the adjoining residences while maintaining all positive off-site views; and to create a low-maintenance beach garden that is sustainable through the use of species indigenous to South Florida in the salt/wind.

Below: View across the water garden. *Dioon spinulosum* flanks the concrete wall designed by the architect.
Bottom: Landscape site plan.

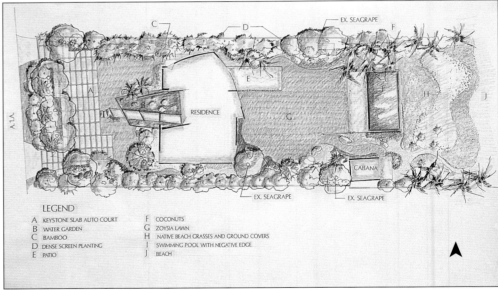

LEGEND

A KEYSTONE SLAB AUTO COURT
B WATER GARDEN
C BAMBOO
D DENSE SCREEN PLANTING
E PATIO
F COCONUTS
G ZOYSIA LAWN
H NATIVE BEACH GRASSES AND GROUND COVERS
I SWIMMING POOL WITH NEGATIVE EDGE
J BEACH

Right: Foreground, *Spathoglottis unguiculata*; middleground, *Dioon spinulosum* and yellow kalanchoe; background, *Bambusa vulgaris*.

Right: A massing of sabal palmetto (the Florida state tree) and pigeon plum screens the adjacent residence. **Far right:** Dune was planted with beach plants such as sea oats, agave, and helianthus.

Design

A native plant barrier was installed along the street to make the property appear to be at the edge of the woods as well as block views of the street and create privacy within the front garden. The overall landscape design was intentionally simple, yet sufficiently bold to play off of the drama of the architecture. The pool was designed with a negative edge to tie into its ocean-front setting. The rear garden was left virtually unplanted along the axis from the main house to the ocean, allowing for the best view of the ocean.

This project was very controversial and high profile while under construction. However, the neighborhood was extremely pleased after completion of the garden since the residence virtually disappeared. This also satisfied the client since she desired a garden with privacy.

Mostly indigenous species are used to look loose and natural and require little maintenance. Some lawn area requires minimal maintenance.

KEY WEST GARDEN

Location: Key West, Florida
Date of Completion: 1997
Owners: Raymond Jungles and Debra Yates
Landscape Architect: Raymond Jungles, Inc.
Landscape Contractor: Plant Creations, Inc.
Lighting: Low voltage Kim and Seagull fixtures
Photography: Lanny Provo
Site Description: One hundred-fifty-by-one-hundred-foot lot with forty year-old native trees
Soils: Three inches of organic topsoil over Keys limestone.
USDA Plant Hardiness Zone: 11
Major Plant Materials: Native species, palms, cycads
Major Hardscape Materials: Concrete, Tikal stone, plywood, recycled greenheart wood
Building Description: The house on this property was originally built by the owner's father from a floor plan in *Better Homes and Gardens* magazine. Jungles and Yates renovated the main house (including major structural repairs). The two-story garage was converted into a two-story cottage that includes vaulted ceilings, an interior staircase, a full kitchen and bath, a sleeping loft, a second-story deck, and a laundry room.
Program: For their own house, the owners wanted to design a garden that can function as two separate private gardens, or as one; and to design and install plant materials which can take prolonged periods of no water or special care.

Previous page: Ceramic mural by Roberto Burle Marx and Haruyoshi Ono projects from a monolithic concrete wall. **Right:** The driveway was converted into a private entry garden for the renovated cottage.

Design

The pool and the garden were designed to accommodate a mural by Roberto Burle Marx and Haruyoshi Ono as well as to create a swimming pool suitable for exercise. The existing 20 x 40-foot pool was twelve inches higher than the finished floor of the main house. Demolition of the pool allowed for the new pool and deck to be built at the same elevation as the house. The new pool is better integrated into the garden while making the garden appear much larger. The location of the mural and the renovations to the main house were orchestrated so that as one enters the front door, the mural dominates the view.

The long driveway was reduced to allow for the creation of a small garden for the cottage which would be private from the rest of the property. A system of walls and fences and an overhead trellis were designed utilizing recycled wood.

Plants native to the Florida Keys were used and selected for their ability to thrive once established in the harsh subtropical climate where rainfall is sporadic if nonexistent for half of the year.

An existing cistern was repaired and is employed specifically for watering the garden. Existing mature trees create a micro-climate and provide heat relief for the understory plantings.

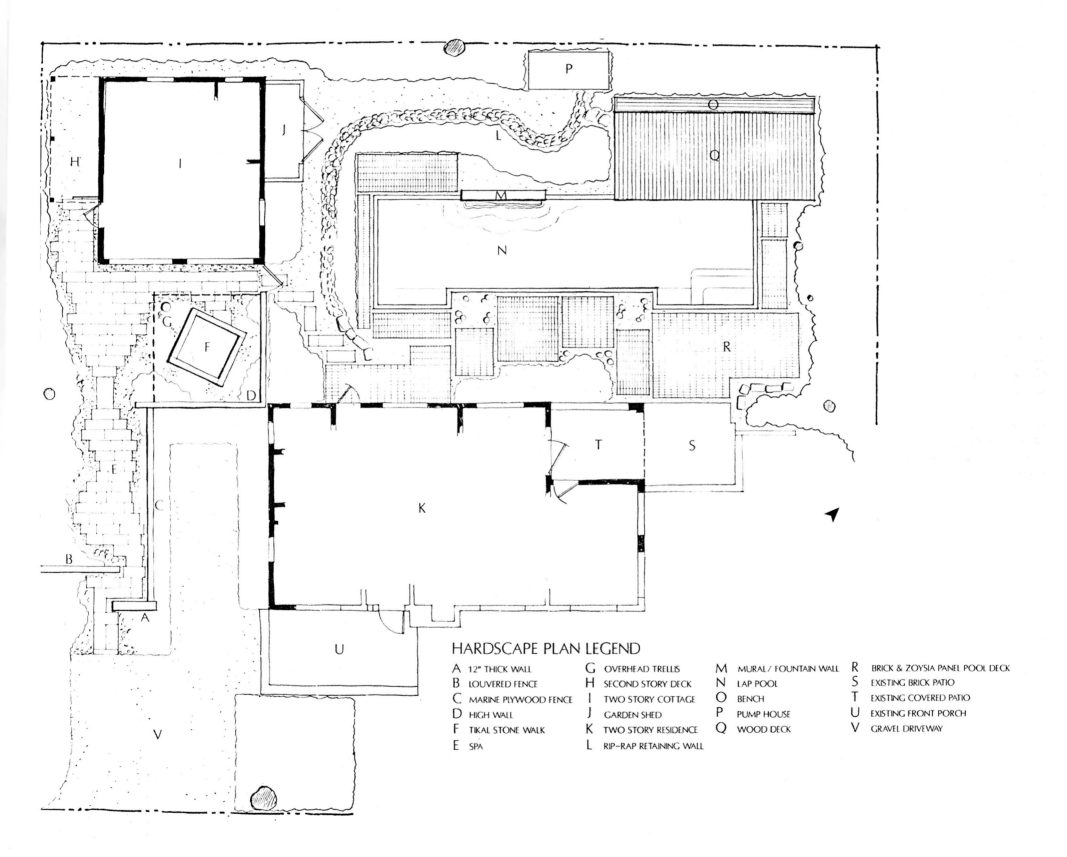

HARDSCAPE PLAN LEGEND

A 12" THICK WALL
B LOUVERED FENCE
C MARINE PLYWOOD FENCE
D HIGH WALL
F TIKAL STONE WALK
E SPA

G OVERHEAD TRELLIS
H SECOND STORY DECK
I TWO STORY COTTAGE
J GARDEN SHED
K TWO STORY RESIDENCE
L RIP-RAP RETAINING WALL

M MURAL / FOUNTAIN WALL
N LAP POOL
O BENCH
P PUMP HOUSE
Q WOOD DECK

R BRICK & ZOYSIA PANEL POOL DECK
S EXISTING BRICK PATIO
T EXISTING COVERED PATIO
U EXISTING FRONT PORCH
V GRAVEL DRIVEWAY

JUNGLES/YATES GARDEN

Location: Miami, Florida
Date of Completion: 1988
Owners: Raymond Jungles and Debra Lynn Yates
Landscape Architects: Raymond Jungles, Inc.
Photography: Lanny Provo
Site Description: The existing site was a typical 100 x 125-foot flat corner lot in a residential area. It had an existing pool and deck. There was no significant character to the architecture. There were a few large existing canopy trees.
Soils: Organic topsoil over oolitic limestone
USDA Plant Hardiness Zone: 10
Major Plant Materials: Native species, palms, cycads, bougainvillea
Major Hardscape Materials: Ceramic mosaic mural walls, mixture of a variety of pavers, galvanized corrugated metal, plywood
Lighting: Low voltage Hadco and Seagull fixtures
Building Description: The building is a one-story residence built in the 1950s. A Florida room was added to the rear of the house and a new bathroom/dressing area was created off of the master bedroom, which has numerous windows facing the garden.
Program: To create a dramatic garden within a limited budget. Converting the existing garage into a design studio and using surplus materials where possible were of particular importance.

Below: The gray-leafed *Bismarckia nobilis* and *Bambusa vulgaris vittata* reflect in the silver gray pool. **Bottom:** The landscape site plan showing a heavy tree canopy. **Right:** View down the entry path to the design studio, formerly a garage.

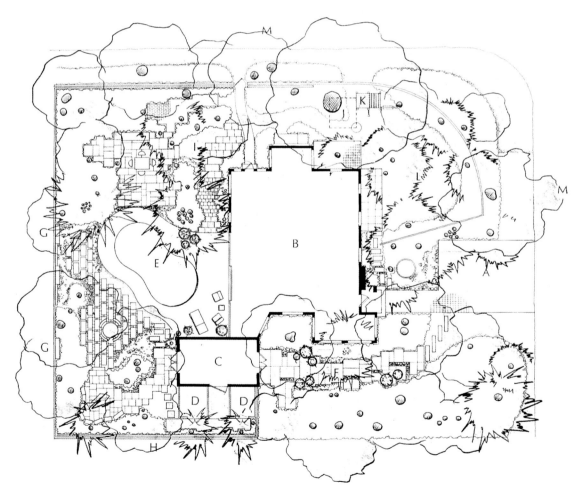

A	AUTO COURT	H	PAINTED PLYWOOD MURAL FENCE
B	RESIDENCE	I	SAND PILE
C	STUDIO	J	TREE HOUSE
D	STORAGE SHEDS	K	PLAY EQUIPTMENT
E	RENOVATED POOL	L	PLAY AREA
F	PATH TO STUDIO	M	STREET
G	MASONRY MURAL WALLS		

Right: Swimming pool and terrace. **Far right:** Foreground, *Zamia furfuracea*; middleground, 5-foot diameter elevated concrete bowl with seasonal color; background, *Neodypsis decaryi*.

Design

The existing pool was resurfaced with a double-silver gray narsite to give it the look of a lagoon, making it highly reflective during the day, bringing the sky into the garden. The existing pool deck was cut into a new, more organic shape and made smaller, allowing for meandering pathways and interesting patios to be built around and adjacent to the pool deck. The garden was heavily planted so that a natural-looking, almost overgrown garden was the result, recalling the landscape architect's visits to the jungles of Brazil.

CORAL GABLES GARDEN

Location: Coral Gables, Florida
Date of Completion: 1996
Owners: Withheld at client's request.
Landscape Architects: Raymond Jungles, Inc.
General Contractor: Action Builders
Landscape Contractor: Plant Creations, Inc.
Consultants: Debra Yates (artist)
Photography: Lanny Provo
Site Description: The existing site was a typical flat 80 x 124-foot lot that contained minimal plantings. One large *Ficus benjamina* was present in the front of the house.
Soils: Organic topsoil over oolitic limestone
USDA Plant Hardiness Zone: 10
Major Plant Materials: Native species, palms, cycads, bougainvillea
Major Hardscape Materials: Ceramic mosaic mural wall, keystone, painted stucco, concrete
Lighting: Low-voltage Hadco, Lumiere, and Kim fixtures
Building Description: The building is a one-story residence built in 1960. Architecturally, there is nothing significant about the structure. The owners, who purchased the house shortly before starting the garden, renovated the interior.
Program: The landscape architect was asked by the client: to design a garden which complemented the residence while creating comfortable exterior spaces that maximize the variety of visual experiences; to contain all off-site views and create privacy; to create garden views from the internal spaces of the residence while integrating the colorful art-filled interior with the garden; to create an entry sequence and backyard recreation areas; to design and integrate a pool, covered outdoor patio, children's play area, and ceramic mosaic mural; to screen the neighboring residences; and to create a low-maintenance, sustainable garden by utilizing species indigenous to South Florida while fulfilling the clients desire for variety, color, and fragrance.

Below: Bromeliads are planted in a trough topping the serpentine mural wall. **Bottom:** The site plan shows the compact areas of the garden. **Right:** A new path meanders through the front garden, connecting the existing driveway with the enlarged front porch.

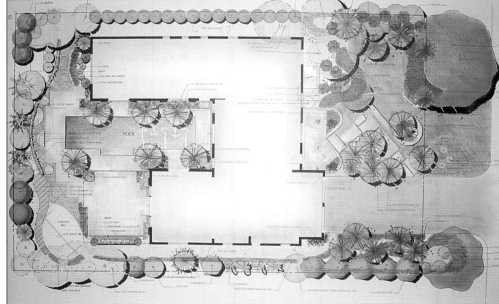

Right: Anthuriums, *Livistona rotundifolia*, and *Thrinax radiata* define the entry path.

Design

The landscape architect worked with the owner to determine a color scheme for the exterior paint and to select all exterior site furnishings. A pool was designed that would maximize the length of the lot as well as views out of the living room. A wall with ceramic mosaic tile was used along most of the back of the property to tie the garden together with color from one end of the house to the other. It also serves to define the edge of the garden. Tall, colorful plantings behind the wall help to create the feeling that the edge of the woods is present behind the wall. The overhead structure designed by the landscape architect helps integrate the interior of the house with the garden and makes the rear of the residence feel like one large room.

This garden demonstrates how to pack a punch into a limited space. Color, water, hardscape elements, vantage points, and an overhead structure were used to create this playful atmosphere. With color reverberating throughout the interior and exterior, an integrated and stimulating environment is present that can be contemplated from many comfortable niches. A pool equipped with jets can become a festive playroom when in use, or a calm reflecting pool when at rest. A variety of hardscape materials have been successfully combined with a diverse collection of rare tropical palms, flowering trees, and indigenous plants, providing an overall sense of richness.

MARATHON GARDEN

Location: Marathon Key, Florida
Date of Completion: 1994
Owners: Withheld at client's request.
Landscape Architects: Raymond Jungles, Inc.
Architect: Mike Beir
General Contractor: Aultman Construction
Landscape Contractor: Plant Creations, Inc.
Consultants: Debra Yates (artist)
Photography: Lanny Provo
Site Description: The existing site was a typical quarter-acre waterfront subdivision lot. The site was flat and contained some generic foundation plantings.
Soils: Limerock fill with some imported planted soil.
USDA Plant Hardiness Zone: 11
Major Plant Materials: Native species, palms, cycads
Major Hardscape Materials: Ceramic mosaic mural walls, fountain, reflecting pool
Lighting: Low-voltage Seagull fixtures
Building Description: One-story building with two-story master wing addition and office/studio addition adjacent to sunken garden.
Program: The owners of this Florida Keys property (a musician and an inventor) decided to build an addition to function as their creative center. They requested that the landscape architect create a setting to feature the art of a ceramic muralist. The challenge was to enliven the small, potentially static space, create drama, and screen the adjacent residential service area.

Right: The mural wall is eight feet high on the garden side but only six feet high on the adjacent property. **Bottom:** Elevation details of the wall.

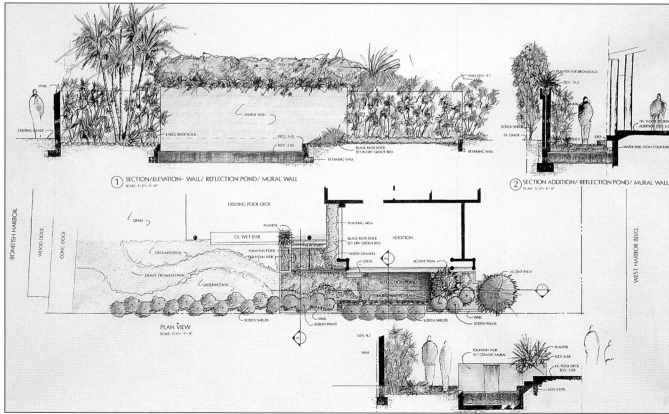

Right: This fountain was designed to feature Debra Yates's art, linking this portion of the garden with the mural wall.

Design

The intent was to design a compact garden space that highlights the work of an artist while maximizing the variety of visual experiences. Due to the compact nature of the garden area and the proximity of a new master bedroom suite to the neighbor's service area, it was necessary to erect a wall of six feet in height by twenty feet in length, two feet from the property line. The wall is eight feet high on the sunken garden side. This wall is both a visual and acoustic barrier that provides a focal point for showcasing the ceramic mosaic mural by Debra Lynn Yates. This "outdoor painting" poised above a reflecting pool brings the sky to the ground, increasing the visual experience from the master bedroom suite. A runnel and waterfall are connected to the reflecting pool and become an element that combines an existing barbecue and pool deck with the new garden space.

This garden requires minimal maintenance.

Raymond Jungles received a bachelor's of landscape architecture degree from the University of Florida in 1981. Upon graduation he obtained his license to practice landscape architecture and began a design/build company, Raymond Jungles, Inc. While at UF, Raymond met Roberto Burle Marx who was lecturing there in 1979. Beginning in 1982, Raymond visited Burle Marx at least once per year, staying at the Sitio and traveling with Roberto on working trips and plant-collecting expeditions. In 1983, Raymond married artist and magazine art director Debra Lynn Yates. Together they have collaborated on several garden projects. Jungles gardens have appeared in numerous publications and have received several design awards. He guest-lectures at the University of Florida and before several garden organizations.

Right: Views to the bay over the fountain. Steps to the right lead to the pool area.

Dan Kiley

CONNECTICUT RESIDENCE

Location: Connecticut

Date of Completion: 1996

Owners: Withheld at client's request.

Landscape Architect: Office of Dan Kiley, Castle Forest, Charlotte, VT 05445.

Design Team: Dan Kiley (principal), Peter Meyer, Richard Pete (project managers), Nanda Patel, Jane P. Amidon, Steve Schenker

Contractor: David Sutton, Sutton Landscape Solutions, and Jim Sutton, Crow and Sutton Landscape

Consultants: Richard Servideo (structural engineer), Richard van Seters (fountains)

Photography: Aaron Kiley

Site Description: Six-hundred plus acres of rolling New England farmland. Historic fragments on site include: orchard; stone walls and farm tracks; old house foundation; outbuildings. Land features include: building site on west-facing slope (oriented towards Taconic Range); intense wind and sun exposure; existing pond and wetland/marsh system.

Soils: Clay/loam

USDA Plant Hardiness Zone: 4-5

Major Plant Materials: *Acer rubrum; Ginkgo biloba; Tilia cordata, Gleditsia triacanthos, Fagus cuprea, Aecsculus hippocastanum, Larix leptolepis, Malus hupehensis, Betula papyrifera, Populus tremuloides, Picea abies, Cornus kousa, Amelanchier canadensis, Syringa amurensis japonica, Magnolia soulangiana, Prunus sargentii, Ilex opaca, Carpinus betula, Cotoneaster horizontalis, Taxus densiformis, Ilex glabra, Euonymous fortunei minima, Vinca minor, Wisteria floribunda, Hydrangea anomala petiolaris;* mixed fern varieties; mixed wild flower varieties.

Major Hardscape Materials: Terrace retaining walls of poured in place concrete with carnelian granite capstones to create seating walls; twenty-four by twenty-four foot carnelian granite with grass joints at entrances, thresholds, and beneath pergolas; canals and fountain pool of black slate tiles with bronze weir; pergola columns are sono-tube-formed concrete with wood members overhead; porte cochere columns are painted steel with steel and glass roofing, crushed stone, and granite below.

Below: Aerial view of the residence and terraces. **Right:** A pair of copper beech trees are silhouetted above the water canal.

Right: A line of littleleaf linden trees leads north to a four-square of chestnut tress at the conservatory. **Far right:** *Wisteria floribunda* and the pergola offer a shady seating area for watching croquet games and sunsets.

Lighting: Tree lights, pergola lights, submerged lighting at fountain

Building Description: A 14,000-square-foot house set on a plinth of retained terrace system. Two stories, with fully finished basement level. Interior swimming pool on south end of house. Wood siding painted white. New tennis court and pavilion.

Program: This is a second home for clients who asked the landscape architect to integrate the house and the land and to provide entertainment and recreation features.

Design

The landscape architect used plant masses (lines, circles, bosques, foursquares, and pairs) and grade manipulation to create spatial structure and to engineer a series of distinct but interconnected volumes. Specific materials are used throughout the site to emphasize continuity and the idea that individual components combine to form a harmonious spatial whole.

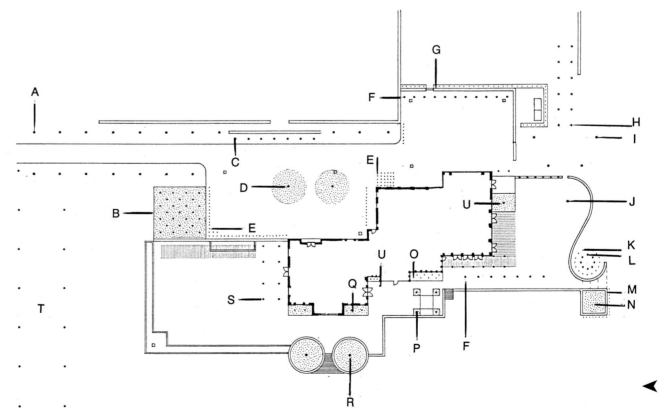

A. *Acer rubrum* allee along entry drive	**G.** *Carpinus betula* clipped hedge at garden entrance and as screen	**M.** *Parthenocissus tricuspidata* along base of retaining walls	**Q.** *Amelanchier canadensis* in cotoneaster bank
B. *Malus hupehensis* bosque set in Vinca and Cotoneaster	**H.** *Crataegus phaenopyrum* allee to tennis court	**N.** Vinca minor at sculpture pad	**R.** *Fagus cuprea* in raised drums, Vinca surface
C. *Ilex opaca*	**I.** *Acer rubrum*	**O.** *Cotoneaster horizontalis* and *Cotoneaster dammeri* 'Skogholm'	**S.** *Gleditsia triacanthos*
D. *Ginkgo biloba* set in Vinca circles at arrival court	**J.** *Larix leptolepis* at curved wall		**T.** Existing apple orchard
E. *Taxus brevifolia*	**K.** *Ilex glabra compacta* circle	**P.** *Aesculus hippocastanum* in Vinca beds	**U.** *Magnolia x soulangiana*
F. *Tilia cordata* line at parking	**L.** *Cornus kousa* circle		

LEHR GARDEN

Location: Miami Beach, Florida
Date of Completion: 1994
Owner: Mira Lehr
Landscape Architect: Office of Dan Kiley
Design Team: Dan Kiley (principal designer)
Lighting: Tree and wall uplights and pergola illumination
Photography: Aaron Kiley, Dan Kiley
Site Description: Small residential lot directly on Indian Creek; existing overgrown shrub and vine layers; existing swimming pool and boat landing.
USDA Plant Hardiness Zone: 9-10
Major Plant Materials: Royal palm, arborvitae, *Wisteria sinensis,* bougainvillea
Major Hardscape Material: Concrete block
Program: This project explores the garden as outdoor living space. The client asked the landscape architect to bring a degree of order and rational sequencing to her comfortable but chaotic quarters.

Design

The landscape architect took his cue from several existing site elements (a partial line of palms at the front door and a rectangular swimming pool) and built a spatial structure off of these. A new bosque of royal palm trees, set eight feet on center, incorporates the existing trees and begins the orderly arrangement of the back area while establishing the composition in relation to the pool. Privacy and a sense of volumetric containment are achieved with eight-foot segments of concrete block wall, covered with flowering vines which parallel the pool's edge.

In a professional career spanning over fifty years, Dan Kiley has worked on some of the country's most important commissions with its most distinguished architects. The recipient of many awards and honors, Dan Kiley's work has been shown at The Museum of Modern Art in New York, The Library of Congress in Washington, D.C., and in traveling national exhibitions.

He has lectured extensively and served on may design juries. His work has been widely published in professional and technical periodicals in the United States and abroad. As one of the country's most eminent landscape architects, Dan Kiley combines experience and imagination with the vision to create classic civic design where building and site come together as one.

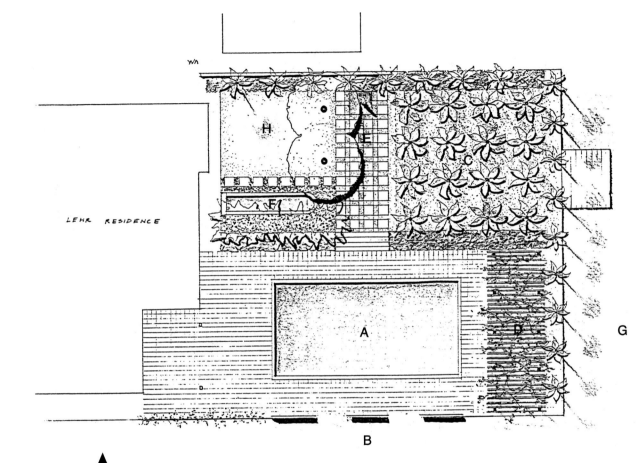

LEHR RESIDENCE

A. Swimming pool with wood plank decking
B. Wall segments with Wisteria screens
C. Royal Palm bosque set in grass
D. Pergola with Wisteria
E. White concrete paving stones set in grass
F. Existing fish pool with grasses and hydrophilic shrubs
G. Canal
H. Grass panel

Top right: Royal palm trees line the front entrance.
Bottom right: Precast concrete pavers with grass joints provide a parking terrace that flows into the adjacent lawn.

Ron Lutsko, Jr.

RANCH SOUTH OF SAN FRANCISCO BAY

Location: South of San Francisco Bay, California
Date of Completion: 1990
Owners: Withheld at client's request.
Landscape Architects: Lutsko Associates, Landscape, Pier 1½, The Embarcadero, San Francisco, CA 94111
Design Team: Ron Lutsko, Jr., Robyn Menigoz
General Contractor: Roger Fiske
Photography: Ron Lutsko, Jr.
Site Description: The garden occupies approximately one-half acre on a large ranch.
Soil: Stony clay
USDA Plant Hardiness Zone: 8
Major Plant Materials: Arctostaphylos, lavandula, salvia, stipa, *Quercus douglasii*
Major Hardscape Materials: Local fieldstone, chocolate sandstone, copper pipe
Building Description: Farmhouse with board and batten siding, covered porches and arbors.
Program: The design intention was to merge this garden with its surroundings which include rolling hills and rock outcroppings. Because the garden is untended for long periods of time, it has been designed to be resilient and self-sustaining. The garden faces deer, frost, minimal water supply, intense summer heat, and occasional cattle, and also must thrive on thin and stony serpentine soils. The composition and the selection of materials are a direct reflection of needs related to these factors.

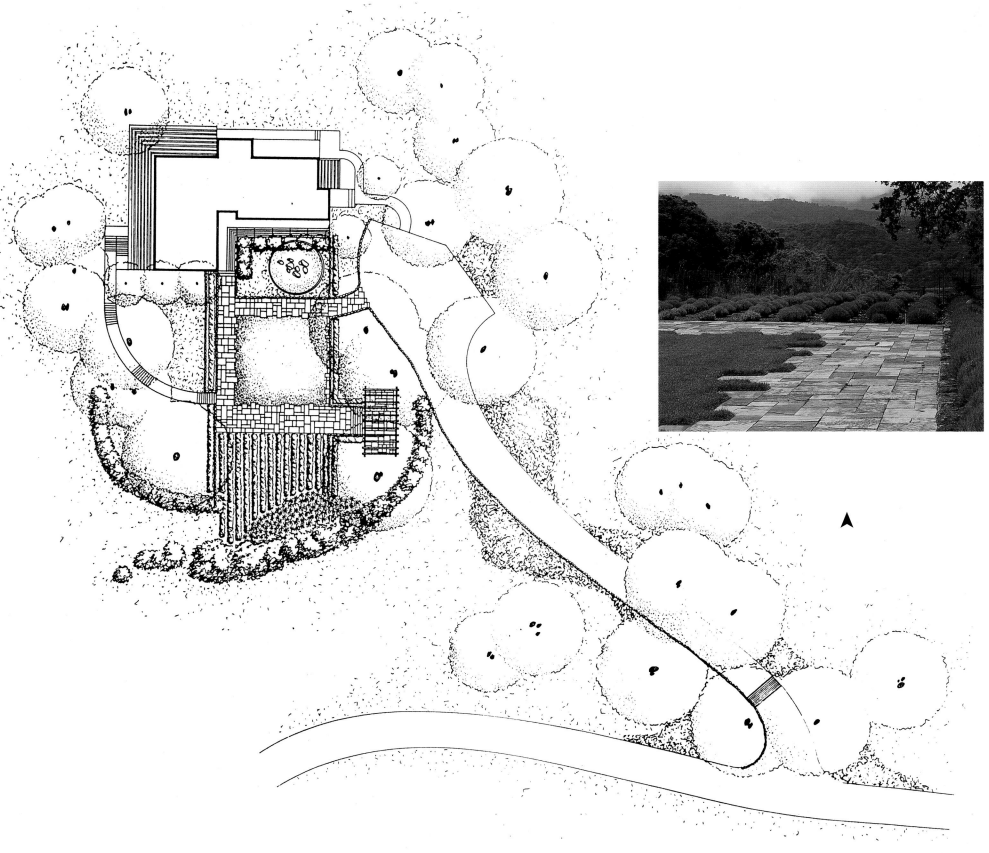

Left: Landscape site plan.
Below: View across garden
with lavender referencing
agrarian land use to the south.

Design

The garden design is based upon four layers of integration moving in succession from the house to the distant landscape. Each layer becomes less formalized as it approaches the wild landscape. The first and most domestic layer is adjacent to the house and is composed of simple geometric patterns, reflecting the form of the building in the garden space. The second layer is a panel of lawn increasing the livability of the garden. Its geometry begins to erode as the edges assume the random pattern of adjacent paving stones. The third layer begins to further connect the garden to the distant landscape by using drought-tolerant ornamentals planted in agrarian rows, reflecting the land use below. The fourth layer becomes the garden edge and is composed of native shrubs, grasses, and flowering herbs arranged to reflect the land forms and plant massing of the natural landscape beyond the site.

Left: View to arbor and house across the lavender field.
Above: Looking west over the lavender field from the arbor.

GREENE GARDEN

Location: St. Helena, California
Date of Completion: 1992
Owners: Marion Greene
Landscape Architect: Lutsko Associates
Design Team: Ron Lutsko, Jr., Eric Blasen
Architect: Kuth/Ranieri with Jim Jennings, Arkhitekture
General Contractor: Cello and Madru, Barry Friesen
Photography: Ron Lutsko, Jr.
Site Description: A three-acre site in the northern
Napa Valley
Soil: Heavy clay
USDA Plant Hardiness Zone: 9
Major Plant Materials: Fruit trees, *Quercus lobata*,
Robinia, *Iris douglasiana*, calamagrostis, stipa, olive
Major Hardscape Materials: Texas limestone, concrete,
galvanized steel, Yosemite tan crushed stone.
Building Description: A 19th-century stone winery
building used for offices, an art gallery, and a private
residence with pool house, guest house, barn, and a light
industrial building.
Program: The client wanted to integrate all of the disparate
parts of the site while at the same time having the landscape
architect create a series of garden spaces, each with a
different character.

Design

The garden is a microcosm of vernacular landscape patterns
found in the Napa Valley. It references the materials and
infrastructure which embody the processes, both natural
and human, that formed the site and its surroundings. The
design maintains the unique quality of each piece of the
site, yet provides a framework to unify the space as a whole.
Water runnels and narrow limestone bands used throughout
the garden provide a visual reference to the network of
irrigation ditches that traverse the Napa Valley. This
acknowledgment addresses the specific source of water for
the site by leading directly to the pump house that is
extracting water from the Napa River. The convergence of
the channels at the center of the site provides a reference
point which renders the disparate portions of the garden
comprehensible and establishes a relationship between all
parts of the site and with the surrounding landscape. The
planting design further emphasizes a connection between
garden and valley by combining vernacular, iconographic
garden plants of the area (olive, cypress, rose, iris) with
regional native plants (bunchgrass, oak, ceanothus, toyon)
and riparian plants specific to the adjacent Napa River.

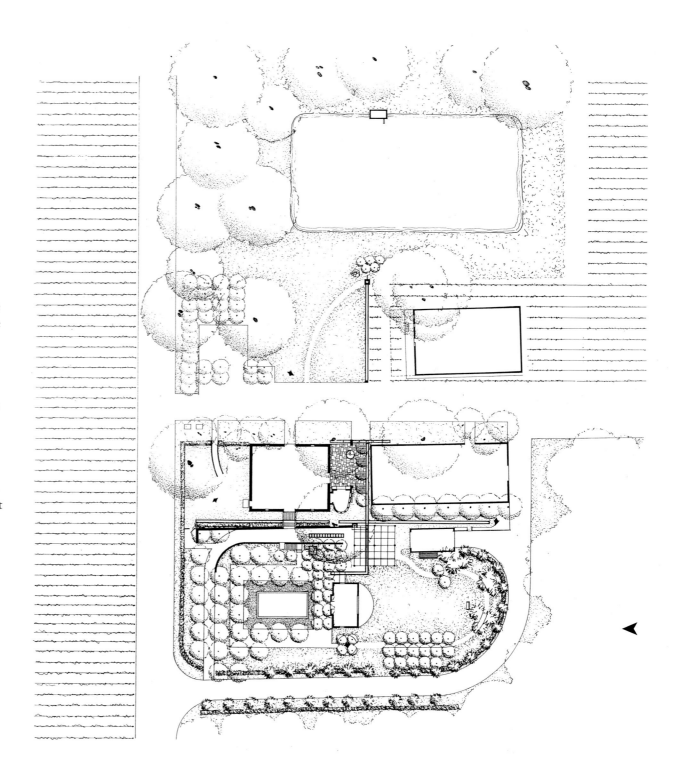

Right: The meeting of water channels at the center of the garden. **Below:** View of the source basin which begins the water system.

Ron Lutsko, Jr., is principal of Lutsko Associates, Landscape, a San Francisco design firm whose projects focus on exploring and expressing the relationship between people and the environment. These projects have been featured in a range of books and magazines and have received numerous local and national awards. Lutsko's educational background includes undergraduate degrees in both horticulture and landscape

architecture from the University of California, Davis, and a graduate degree in landscape architecture from the University of California, Berkeley. He now teaches in the landscape architecture departments of both schools.

Clockwise from top: Outdoor gallery courtyard from the office window; view up runnel from gallery court to pump house; looking down on *Quercus alba* in the gallery court.

Steve Martino

DeBARTOLO GARDEN

Location: Paradise Valley, Arizona
Date of Completion: 1993
Owners: Jack and Pat DeBartolo, Jr.
Landscape Architect: Steve Martino & Associates, 3336 32nd Street, Suite 110, Phoenix, AZ 85018
Design Team: Steve Martino and Jack DeBartolo, Gary Slater (sculptor)
Architect: Jack DeBartolo, Jr.
General Contractor: T.P. Collins Construction
Photography: Steve Martino
Site Description: Eastern oriented hillside with 17° slope
Soil: Rocky
USDA Plant Hardiness Zone: 13
Major Plant Materials: Native plants and turf
Major Hardscape Materials: Concrete, boulders
Lighting: Accent ground lighting
Building Description: This desert residence, designed by the architect for himself and his wife, is a contemporary, minimalist, one-room house with a free plan. The design incorporates year-round living space for the couple and seasonal guest accommodations for their family.
Program: The landscape architect was asked to create a landscape that skillfully mimics the indigenous flora of the high desert creating an integral relationship between the house and its site to the surrounding desert.

Below left: View from the upper level porch to the offset pattern of the pool, terrace, and fountain with the punctured wall framing the mountain views to the east. The southern wall serves as rule for the hillside, terminating the terrace space. **Right:** The concept of the garden is one of connection to the desert with the reflected colonnade acting as an extension of the architectural order. The garden also becomes the mediator between the designed and natural desert forms.

Right: Rising from guest parking, the garden becomes legi-
ble as it orients one to the
overall site context with the
pool and wall below as focus.
Below: Landscape site plan.

Design

The design investigation immediately focused on the site, a
cresting hillside with slopes approaching twenty percent,
eastern exposure, and access from below. After analyzing
view corridors, distant vistas, climate, and solar issues, a
major west wall emerged as the primary organizing element,
shielding the living spaces from the harsh western sun and
delineating a commanding line in the landscape. The upper
terrace, introduced as a new ground plane, allows unlimited
connection to the outdoors. The unobstructed views to the
north, east, and south make the experience of the house, in
its extraordinary context, much richer than photographs
can capture.

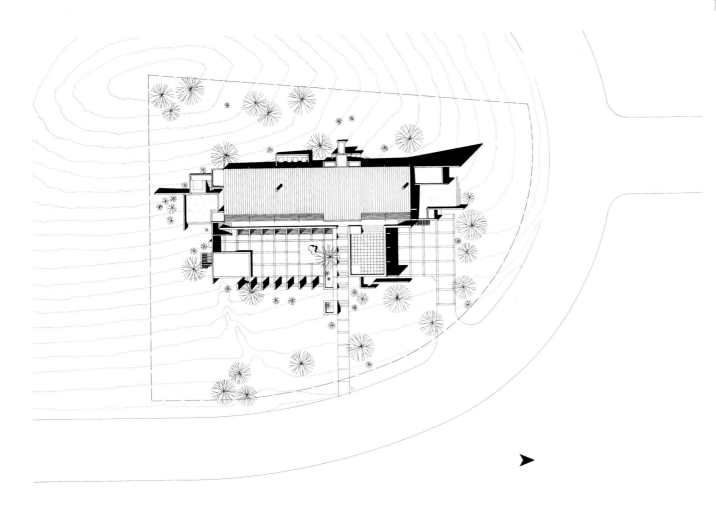

HILLSIDE RESIDENCE

Location: Phoenix, Arizona
Date of Completion: 1996
Owners: Withheld at client's request.
Landscape Architect: Steve Martino & Associates
Design Team: Steve Martino (principal designer)
Architect: Douglas Architecture & Planning
General Contractor: R.J. Bromley Construction
Lighting: Steve Martino
Photography: Steve Martino
Site Description: Hillside
Soil: Rocky
USDA Plant Hardiness Zone: 13
Major Plant Materials: Native plants
Major Hardscape Materials: Porous, decomposed granite, steel, stucco
Building Description: A remodeled 1950s contemporary house
Program: The clients, who have three small children, hired the landscape architect to develop functional outdoor living spaces along with a native plant habitat landscape that would invite wildlife to be part of their garden.

Design

The site was governed by a new hillside ordinance permiting no new grading. The existing pool and deck took up virtually the entire usable back yard. The landscape architect removed them, allowing the space to become a large outdoor room. The existing concrete walks, asphalt parking, and drive as well as nonnative plant materials were removed. The original hard paving was replaced with porous decomposed granite. Transparent steel gates were designed for security without being inhospitable and the auto court was positioned to create a buffer from the street. The yellow retaining wall was built at the back of the existing planter, making the usable space in the outdoor room four feet wider while removing the unattractive slope directly above the planter. The yellow color selected for the wall is the dominate flower color of the native landscape of the hillside beyond.

Below: Stairway from the master bedroom terrace to the upper picnic and nature area.

The stairs lead to an uphill area that overlooks the house to the distant views beyond. The concrete counter/kids art table seats ten. The small fountain doubles as a wading pool. It has a removable stainless steel screen set one inch below the water for toddler safety. The existing building pad at the east terrace was reworked to create the arroyo garden outside the living room. The shallow reflection trough at the far end of the patio slab doubles as a play area for the kids; boulders are placed for their use as tables and chairs.

The garden has been designed for the children's use as much as for the adult's use. The hardscape evolved from attempting to meet both the client's program requirements and difficult site problems. The native plants used relate the landscape back to the underlying native landscape and character of the region, demonstrating that habitat-building native plants are not only acceptable as landscape material but are an important alternative to the conventional nature-displacing exotic plants that are so frequently used in landscape architecture.

Above: Entry gates and storage enclosure as seen from the edge of the street. **Right, clockwise from top left:** Gates and storage enclosure in auto court; entry path and steps at the entry terrace; the gate from the auto court to the entry pathway; and glass tile wading pool and fountain.

HAWKINSON GARDEN

Location: Phoenix, Arizona
Date of Completion: 1993
Owners: Jay Hawkinson
Landscape Architect: Steve Martino & Associates
Design Team: Steve Martino (principal designer)
Photography: Steve Martino
Site Description: A small corner lot in a development where all houses and site walls visible to the street are required to be painted white. The site backs up to an open-space drainage wash area.
Soil: Rocky
USDA Plant Hardiness Zone: 13
Major Plant Materials: Native plants
Major Hardscape Materials: Plaster, Plexiglas, crushed stone
Building Description: Single-family house
Program: The client, a corporate art director, requested a garden refuge. The landscape architect expanded the client's program beyond just solving the typical functional and site restraint issues and attempted to create a garden that expressed solar, cultural, social, and ecological connections with the region.

Below: Grand steps between garden levels. **Right:** View to the lower garden level from the dining patio.

Design

Located in a city whose existence is based on denial of the desert, the garden seeks to connect its inhabitants with the spirit of the desert, both past and present. The fountain walls diagram a man with open arms embracing the morning sun. The water channel aligns with the axis of the sunrise on the summer solstice.

This garden is a cultural expression of the client's personality. Woven into this cultural landscape is a strong representation of regional ecology. The landscape is regenerative in that the native plant material is self-perpetuating and the rain runoff is captured to benefit the plants. Native plants link this garden directly to the ecological processes of the site and region.

The fountain helps diminish adjacent traffic noise. The curved walls focus the waters' sound back to the patio and mask the fussiness of the existing development's wall. The water channel is the passageway to the secret rooms (outdoor shower and storage). The red Plexiglas construction joint is the terminus of the water channel passageway. It is illuminated by sunlight and backlit at night.

The blue pyramid functions as a cardinal focal point from the hallway axis in the house. The lower level is sunken into the earth not unlike the ruins of a great kiva. This technique lowers the finish grade and provides greater separation from the street noise. Wall colors were created on site by trial and error by adding pigment to the plaster.

Steve Martino, FASLA, has earned a national reputation for design excellence in landscape architecture. His pioneering work with native plant material and the development of a desert-derived aesthetic is widely recognized. This innovative spirit on behalf of the desert has earned him more than seventy-five local, regional, and national design awards. His designs have been published in nearly two hundred books and periodicals. His work has ranged from urban development to remote large-scale communities to private gardens. (Photo: Dillon Martino)

Randall K. Metz

NORM AND HARRIET'S GARDEN

Location: Birmingham, Michigan
Date of Completion: 1992
Owners: Norm and Harriet Rotter
Landscape Architect: Grissim/Metz Associates, Inc., 37801
Twelve Mile Road, Farmington Hills, MI 48331
Design Team: Randall K. Metz, ASLA (principal in charge
of design)
Architect: Neumann/Smith Associates, Southfield, MI
General Contractor: Wineman and Komer Building Co.,
Southfield, MI
Consultants: C. J. Colein Associates (irrigation design)
Lighting: Low-voltage and line-voltage uplighting,
sculpture lighting, pathway lighting
Photography: Balthazar Korab Ltd.
Site Description: Two-acre suburban property, densely
wooded, poorly drained
Soil: Clay
USDA Plant Hardiness Zone: 4
Major Plant Materials: White pine, *Vinca minor*, various
perennials (i.e., hosta, astilbe), ornamental grasses
Major Hardscape Materials: Sandstone retaining walls,
black rustic terrazzo
Building Description: One-story contemporary house
with living spaces organized around a single circulation
spine strongly expressed in the architectural composition.
The house is painted white both inside and out, to contrast
with the natural setting and to serve as a backdrop for the
client's extensive art collection.
Program: Densely wooded with mature white pine trees,
the suburban two-acre site presented unique design
challenges for both the architect and landscape architect.
Soils were heavy and poorly drained, and surface runoff was
minimal; consequently pockets of small wooded wetlands
had collected along the eastern boundary. The western edge
of the site parallels a heavily used collector highway, and
traffic noise is extremely invasive.

The clients are successful professionals with an enthusiastic
commitment to promoting the arts. They regard
architecture and landscape architecture as inseparable art
forms and formulated the following design goals for the
site: preserve the existing trees; protect and enhance the
natural beauty of the site; develop a unique and artful
landscape solution; and visually unite architecture,
landscape architecture, and the natural environment.

Design

In order to achieve these design objectives, concepts for the
house and site were developed as a collaborative effort by
the architect and landscape architect. The design and
orientation of the house was a response to the client's design
goals and to off-site traffic noise. Spaces within the house
are organized along a central spine that divides living spaces
from the garage and mechanical rooms. Functioning as a

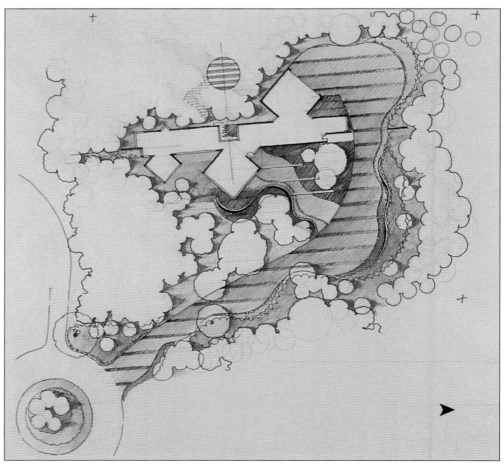

Top left: View south adjacent to the living room from the entry walk. **Bottom left:** Landscape site plan. **Top:** View looking west towards the house entry. **Right:** View from the vestibule of the house.

noise deflector, the central axis of the house is ideal for art display and establishes a linear framework for the building's architecture.

Site circulation presented a challenge due to existing tree locations and the designer's desire to avoid a textbook solution to the driveway configuration. In its conception the drive was envisioned as a "paved river" transversing the site while meandering around major trees and small wetland areas. The larger undulations create sufficient space for visitor parking. To visually unite the driveway with the architecture, a bold pattern of lines was painted on the surface in keeping with to the linear architectural concept of the house.

A black-and-white color scheme was used exclusively throughout the site and house to create a neutral background for interior and exterior art display. Specific locations were integrated into the landscape and architecture for display of sculpture by David Barr.

The entrance walk, a rustic terrazzo composed of black marble and sand, is broadly terraced and is an extension of the driveway concept. Concrete steps are on the same module as the driveway stripe pattern and extend the theme to the front door of the house.

Inspired by the flowing forms of the driveway and the house's strong architectural statement, the landscape design commanded an equally bold response. Ribbons of plant material run through the site accentuating the organic form of the driveway. Strategically placed white pine trees extend the indigenous vegetation to areas requiring additional buffering. Plant varieties were chosen for their white flowers or white variegated foliage to reinforce the black-and-white color scheme established by the architecture. Extensive subsurface drainage measures were used to enable large perennial beds to thrive in the poorly drained soils. Natural stone retaining walls complement the naturalized planting forms, preserve existing trees, and present the house at a consistent grade elevation.

KAUFMAN GARDEN

Location: Bloomfield Hills, Michigan
Date of Completion: 1995
Owners: Alan and Sue Ellen Kaufman
Landscape Architect: Grissim/Metz Associates, Inc.
Design Team: Randall Metz, ASLA, Sue Grissim, ASLA
Architect: Neuman/Smith Associates, Southfield, MI
General Contractor: Sue's Landscape, Inc.
Consultants: C.J. Colein Associates (irrigation design)
Photography: Randall Metz
Site Description: Two-acre rolling suburban property with existing home and large trees
Soil: Clay
USDA Plant Hardiness Zone: 4
Major Plant Materials: White birch, green spruce, Scotch pine, myrtle, perennials, bulbs
Major Hardscape Materials: Redwood decking, concrete brick paving
Lighting: Landscape up and down lighting
Building Description: Existing two-story contemporary home with new family room and master bedroom addition.
Program: To provide outdoor living spaces that will accommodate large gatherings or small family events. The program also included a tennis court.

Design

The principle concept organizes circulation around a single linear spine linking various access points of the house at different elevations. The spine terminates in a "window" which frames a specimen Scotch pine. Planting defines the spine and creates the outdoor spaces. White birch trees contrast with the dark color of the house, and a variety of flowering shrubs, perennials, and bulbs provide seasonal color (i.e., viburnum, azalea, hostra, astilbe, and tulips). Terraces with concrete brick paving establish the ground plane, while redwood decking accommodates the above-grade access locations.

Randall K. Metz, ASLA is principal and director of design of Grissim/Metz Associates Inc. He received his bachelor of landscape architecture from Michigan State University in 1976.

Left: View adjacent to the family room. **Right:** View along the linear axis.

Robert Murase

PRIVATE RESIDENCE

Location: Woodside, California
Date of Completion: 1990
Owners: Withheld at client's request.
Landscape Architect: Murase Associates, Inc. 1300 NW Northrup Street, Portland, OR 97209; 320 Terry Avenue North, Seattle, WA 98109
Design Team: Robert K. Murase (principal designer)
Landscape Contractor: Jim Lord; Paul Discoe (carpenter)
Photography: Murase Associates, Inc.
Site Description: Located south of San Francisco, this existing 5-acre estate is characterized by a grouping of mature California live oaks.
Soil: Sandy/loam
USDA Plant Hardiness Zone: 9
Major Plant Materials: San Francisco Bay area native plants
Major Hardscape Materials: Sandstone terraces, walkways, walls
Building Description: The house was designed by Joseph Eshrick in the 1950s.
Program: The site lies in a small valley on a peninsula south of San Francisco. Over 100 densely growing California live oak trees created a very dark garden. The irrigation needs of the existing garden, primarily ornamental plants and lawn areas, were causing a fungus disease to grow on the oak tree roots. It was decided that the oak trees would be carefully pruned to let light filter in, and the existing garden would be replaced with native San Francisco Bay area plants.

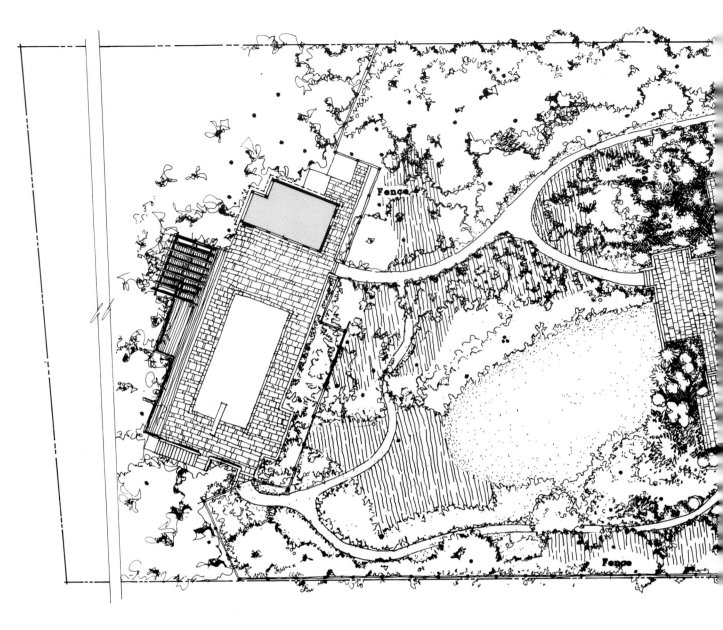

Above: Landscape site plan. **Left:** Entry fences and pergola off the auto court. **Right:** Partial view of the house from the gravel terrace. **Far right:** Swimming pool area paved with sandstone and planted with California native plants.

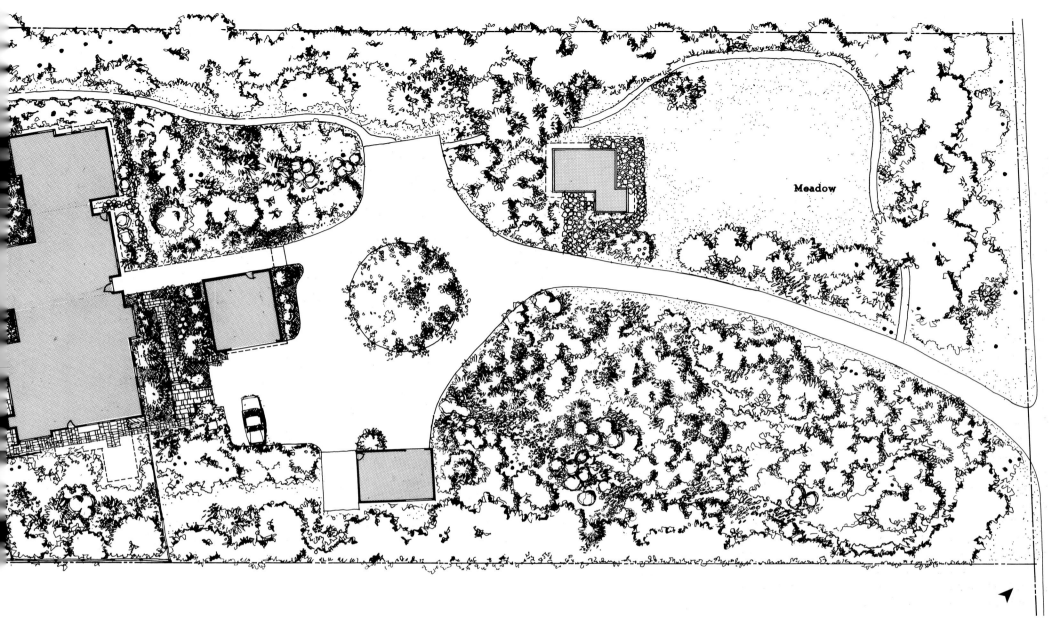

Meadow

Top left: View from the living room terrace. **Bottom left:** View of the stone terrace with a sandstone water basin. **Right:** Graveled area beneath california live oak trees and coffeeberry trees.

Design

The intent was to create a quiet, elegant garden by seeking timeless design solutions. The client was very open to the landscape architect's ideas and aesthetic directions. With the freedom to explore a diversity of design ideas, the landscape architect was able to discover wonderful outdoor living places, provocative visual landscapes, and gardens of shadowed reflections.

New terraces and courtyards were developed off the living and bedroom areas and the main entrance to the house. These spaces were built with sandstone walls, steps, and paving delineating the edges of the formal living areas. Edges demarcating entryways were also defined by fences, gateways, and an arbor. The carpenter, Paul Discoe, who trained in temple carpentry in Japan, crafted these pieces with exquisite joinery and refinement. A swimming pool and terrace were developed with an arbor, which terminates a connecting trail around the property. A barn was converted into a maintenance building, and a meadow and play area were created for the client's grandchildren.

An internationally recognized landscape architect, Robert Murase has more than thirty years' experience working in the United States, Japan, the Pacific Basin, and the Caribbean. As principal of Murase Associates, he has completed a wide array of projects including university campuses, visitor and resort complexes, new town facilities, and parks and recreation facilities. Mr. Murase has a strong reputation for designing special places with a dedication to craft that becomes art, and has won numerous awards for his work. He is the subject of a recently published book by Spacemaker Press, Robert Murase: Stone and Water *(1997).*

Mark Rios

SCHRADER-BOHNETT GARDEN

Location: Los Angeles, California
Date of Completion: 1991
Owners: Rand Schrader and David Bohnett
Landscape Architect: Rios Associates, Inc., 8008 West 3rd Street, Los Angeles, CA 90048.
Design Team: Mark Rios (principal), Julie Smith (project architect)
Architect: Rios Associates, Inc.
General Contractor: McCord Construction, Santa Monica, CA
Photography: Dominique Vorillon, Rios Associates
Site Description: A steeply sloping hillside site in the Santa Monica Mountains.
Soil: Decomposed granite
USDA Plant Hardiness Zone: 10
Major Plant Materials: *Eucalyptus citriodora,* melaleuca, *Dietes vegeta, Cotoneaster horizontalis, Rosmarinus officinalis,* cistus, salvia
Major Hardscape Materials: Exposed aggregate concrete, slate, tile
Building Description: The original architecture of this tract home borrowed from the Case Study houses of Southern California. When it was remodeled, the architect sought to strengthen those elements that embodied formal ideas from the Case Study movement such as opening up the rear of the house and dissolving the separation between interior and exterior spaces.
Program: Program elements included a new entry walk, all stairs and railings, modifications to the house including incorporation of a new koi pond around a new floor-to-ceiling corner window, pool and deck, retaining walls, fountains, trellises, hardscape elements, lighting, and plant materials.

Design

This project exemplifies the power of landscape design to extract a simple idea from an existing building as a source of form making. The landscape design solution personifies an ideology that the original building never achieved: the contrast between deliberate, built geometries and the rougher texture of the hillside to maintain a balance between civilization and nature.

The entry garden provides design cues that are unveiled throughout the project. Architectural layers are added to the front of the residence to create a sense of depth and scale. Geometric forms such as the front curved-tile entry wall extend the architectural forms into the landscape. A pool of water begins inside the house and is extended through a glass corner window into the garden.

Below: Landscape site plan.
Bottom: A tiled retaining wall creates a shimmering edge along the pool, separating the living areas of the backyard from the native hillside beyond. **Right:** The spa fountain provides a garden focal point.

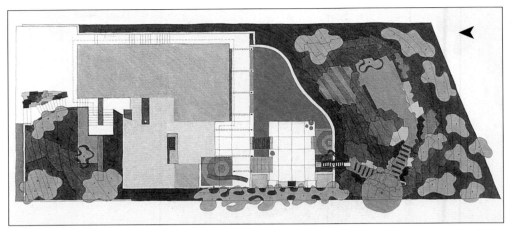

Below right: Custom-
designed outdoor furniture
echoes the garden's curving
forms. **Bottom right:** Plants
embrace the hillside steps.

The undulating tiled retaining wall at the base of the hill in
the back garden defines the larger hardscape area and also
serves as the rear wall of the swimming pool. The pool is
multi-functional, allowing for lap swimming, recreational
play, and seating. Within the pool there is a spa with a
fountain in the form of an ascending column, providing a
strong focal point. The paved deck connects the pool to the
hill beyond and provides a barbecue area and space for
outdoor entertaining.

A hillside terrace was developed into a secondary garden
space. This garden is reached by a metal stairway which
pierces the curved retaining wall and leads to two flights of
railroad tie steps. Providing an intimate and private area,
this space commands dramatic views of the surrounding
hillsides.

Plantings consist of drought-tolerant indigenous material,
in context with the nature of the surrounding hills which
spill down into the pool area, effectively connecting the
house with its surroundings.

COLLECTOR'S GARDEN

Location: Southern California
Date of Completion: 1995
Owners: Withheld at client's request.
Landscape Architects: Rios Associates, Inc.
Design Team: Mark Rios (principal-in-charge), Charles Pearson (principal), Polly Furr (project landscape architect), Dale Wall, Frank Clementi, Julie Smith, Hsuan-Ying Chou
Architect: Frank Gehry, Langdon Wilson Architecture Planning
General Contractor: Owner
Consultants: Courtland Paul, FASLA (consulting landscape architect), Spindler Engineering (civil engineering), Herman Goodman & Associates, Inc. (fountain/pool structural engineering), Pacific Water Designs (fountain mechanical engineering), Associated Irrigation Consultants (irrigation design), Calligari & Associates (tree broker), John Greenlee, Greenlee Nursery (plant selection consultant)
Photography: Dominique Vorillon, Rios Associates
Site Description: A long, narrow lot on the steep western slope of a south-facing canyon.
Soils: Heavy clay with rocky areas and some decomposing sandstone
USDA Plant Hardiness Zone: 10
Major Plant Materials: *Schinus molle, Phormium cookianum* (New Zealand flax), *Ficus rubiginosa, Acanthus mollis, Philodendron evansii, Cistus* sp., *Trachelospermum jasminoides, Podocarpus* sp.
Major Hardscape Materials: Pennsylvania bluestone, stainless steel, Beruli sandstone, seeded exposed aggregate concrete, crushed stone
Building Description: Entered from a stainless steel and sandstone sculpture court, the house is composed of second-floor living spaces over a gallery, loggia, and guest house below. Crowned by a roof of curving steel plates, its sculptural form is art in its own right. The house serves as an environment for displaying pieces from the owner's extensive contemporary art collection.
Program: The client's internationally recognized interest in collecting contemporary art provided an opportunity to view the landscape in a new way, creating a design that is a unique expression of place while developing functional outdoor spaces that frame and participate in the art experience. The constraints of the site, including challenging utility easements, dramatic topography, and a long and narrow lot configuration, acted as catalysts for, rather than barriers to, design.

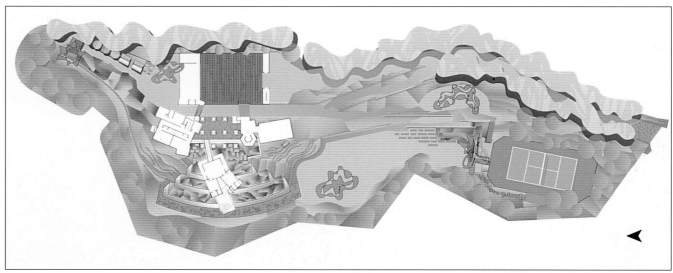

Right, clockwise from top:
Stonework details; "lake water" is recirculated through a crushed stone walkway; detail of runnel at fountain and stair.

Design

Development of a myth of place helped to create a space of visceral character for the architecture to inhabit. The powerful scale of the building's architecture required that the landscape respond with a strength of its own to avoid being lost, or to risk trivializing the architecture with "decoration." Traditional elements of the garden were exaggerated, including the edgeband, perennial garden, crushed stone path, and stone wall.

At the estate's main entry, a stainless steel gate slips open across a stone platform to reveal an allée of California pepper trees which close over a curved, crushed stone seeded drive. The drive offers glimpses of the gardens below and a dramatic view of the house before terminating at the enclosed sculpture court.

The house stands partially in a ziggurat-shaped "lake."
A thin line of water drops over each lake terrace, falling into a crushed stone pathway on the lowest terrace level, The lake's east stairs open to the lawn, which counterbalances the massive forms of the house and site walls with its open expanse. A swimming pool sits at the western edge of the lawn, tucked against terraces which climb against natural rock outcroppings. A mammoth border planting of New Zealand flax forms an undulating edge to the lawn, and continues along the walkway at the base of the lake, unifying the entire southern perimeter.

On the west side of the lake, crushed stone pathways border gardens which hug the steep slope. The bank falls away into an oversized perennial border, which is placed on the slope where its scale and color can be appreciated from the house.

Respecting the microclimates of the site, the lawn is located in the most sheltered area. Slopes are planted with a mix of drought-tolerant shrubs and ground covers appropriate for a dry hillside. Crushed stone pathways, plant-filled joints in the driveway, and permeable parking surfaces are all designed to reduce runoff. The lake is recirculated through the crushed stone walkway on the lowest terrace level, using a specially designed biological filtration system.

Rios Associates, Inc. is foremost a design office of dedicated, creative individuals with diverse education and backgrounds. Collectively, the combined talents of the office comprise a wide range of professional skills including architecture, landscape architecture, interior and furniture design.

Right: A trough of water creates a reveal, holding the sandstone paving back from the stainless steel wall of the sculpture court.

CALIFORNIA LANDSCAPE

Location: Los Angeles, California
Date of Completion: Ongoing
Owners: Withheld at client's request.
Landscape Architect: Achva Benzinberg Stein & Associates, 1116 Diamond Avenue, South Pasadena, California 91030
Design Team: Achva Benzinberg Stein (principal designer)
Architect: Donald Polsky, 1956; Smith-Miller + Hawkinson, 1989-91; Smith-Miller + Hawkinson, extension, 1997-98
General Contractor: Naturescape
Photography: Tim Street-Porter
Site Description: The house straddles a ridge with dramatic vistas of the Pacific Ocean and Los Angeles to the west and the San Gabriel Mountains and the San Bernardino Mountains to the east. The new extension is on a steep hillside that drops precipitously to the southwest.
Soils: Decomposed granite, alkaline, low organic content, poor in nutrients
USDA Plant Hardiness Zone: 10
Major Plant Materials: California natives and drought-tolerant Mediterranean plants
Major Hardscape Materials: Decomposed granite, stone, pressure-treated timber
Building Description: Inspired by the Case Study houses, the layout of the house merges the interior spaces with the dramatic ridge-top setting.
Program: Develop a low-maintenance naturalized garden; extend the living space of the house; present panoramic views in a series of contrasting experiences, borrowing images of the California landscape; and connect the "inaccessible" areas of the property.

Design

A series of contained gardens are organized by the geometry of the architecture and the programmatic functions of the house, responding to specific environmental conditions. The front yard strongly echoes the rectilinear planes of the house with seasonal plantings, constantly refocusing the viewer's attention while framing the distant mountains. The backyard extends the living spaces of the house out along a subtly shifting ground plane that incorporates water, hardscape, mounded fescue grasses, and a sculptured pine tree. A grove of melaleucas with peeling silver bark creates an outdoor eating and gathering place on the kitchen side

Below: Plan of the front garden. **Right:** View from front entry overlooking courtyard garden with wisteria arbor and San Gabriella mountains in the distance.

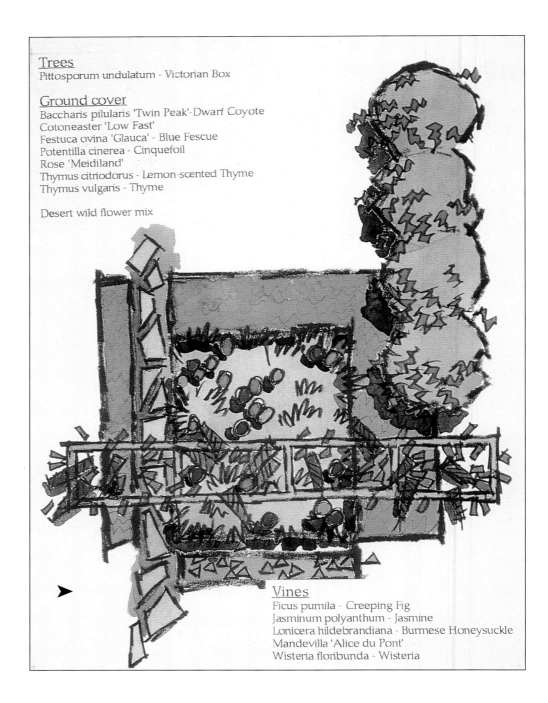

Trees
Pittosporum undulatum - Victorian Box

Ground cover
Baccharis pilularis 'Twin Peak'-Dwarf Coyote
Cotoneaster 'Low Fast'
Festuca ovina 'Glauca' - Blue Fescue
Potentilla cinerea - Cinquefoil
Rose 'Meidiland'
Thymus citriodorus - Lemon-scented Thyme
Thymus vulgaris - Thyme

Desert wild flower mix

Vines
Ficus pumila - Creeping Fig
Jasminum polyanthum - Jasmine
Lonicera hildebrandiana - Burmese Honeysuckle
Mandevilla 'Alice du Pont'
Wisteria floribunda - Wisteria

of the house. The dappled light in the strong southern exposure is sufficient for herbs to creep between the flagstones. The shady north garden is completely enclosed and private. Baby tears, ferns, camellias, abutilons, and a bamboo backdrop shield this retreat from the intense California sun.

The plantings, while using a modernist vocabulary of abstracted planes and rectilinear forms, never lose their connection to sensory pleasure or utility. The simple layout derives in part from an agrarian sensibility.

The contained gardens contrast to the larger naturalized hillside where the structure and organization of the landscape respond to the hydrologic conditions and microclimates created by the changing aspects and elevation of the slope. A series of steps link paths traversing the hillside on grade at different elevations. The paths connect a series of distinct plant communities, from chaparral along the exposed upper reaches to oak woodland at the bottom. Also included are a small citrus grove and vegetable garden. A sitting platform under a small grove of oaks is the terminus of an exhibition that leads the stroller to focus inward, away from the panoramic view into the blue flowering salvia. Blue flowering bulbs, including iris, hyacinths, and blue anemones framed by white trailing roses, evoke memories of seasonal California brooks. All plant material is selected for its water-conservation qualities. Only the area immediately surrounding the pool is planted with a traditional lawn.

Ms. Stein is both a practicing landscape architect and director of the graduate program in landscape architecture in the School of Architecture at the University of Southern California. She holds a Master of Landscape Architecture from Harvard University and a Bachelor of Landscape Architecture from the University of California at Berkeley. She has taught and

practiced in the United States, Israel, Europe, India, and China. Her work and writings have appeared in Landscape Architecture, Arquitectura Viva, ID, The New York Times *and* The Los Angeles Times. *She was awarded the Chrysler Award for Innovation in Design in 1995.*

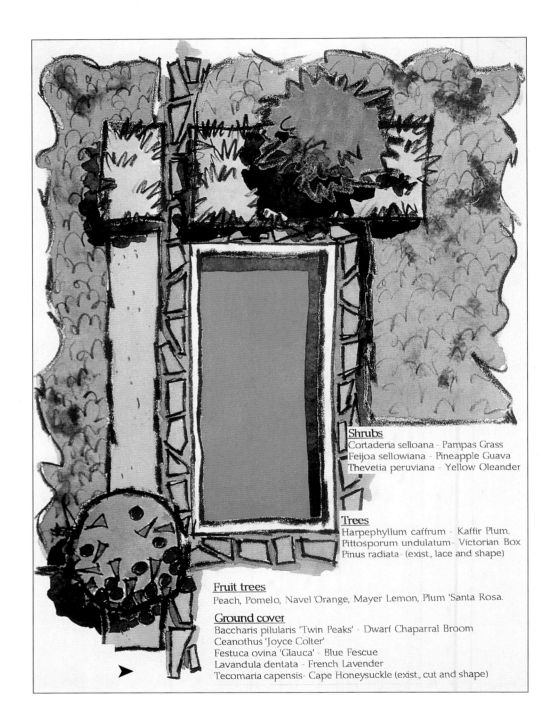

Shrubs
Cortaderia selloana - Pampas Grass
Feijoa sellowiana - Pineapple Guava
Thevetia peruviana - Yellow Oleander

Trees
Harpephyllum caffrum - Kaffir Plum.
Pittosporum undulatum - Victorian Box
Pinus radiata - (exist., lace and shape)

Fruit trees
Peach, Pomelo, Navel 'Orange, Mayer Lemon, Plum 'Santa Rosa.

Ground cover
Baccharis pilularis 'Twin Peaks' - Dwarf Chaparral Broom
Ceanothus 'Joyce Colter'
Festuca ovina 'Glauca' - Blue Fescue
Lavandula dentata - French Lavender
Tecomaria capensis - Cape Honeysuckle (exist., cut and shape)

Gary Leonard Strang

LEE'S ORCHARD

Location: Milpitas, California
Date of Completion: 1992
Owners: Lee's Orchard Homeowner's Association
Landscape Architect: Gary Leonard Strang, GLS Architect/Landscape Architect, 246 First Street, #400, San Francisco, CA 94106
Design Team: Gary Strang (landscape architect), Barbara Stauffacher Solomon (artist)
Architect: Daniel Solomon and Kathryn Clarke
Developer: Green Rock Corp., John Schink, President
Photography: Gary Strang
Site Description: A 10-acre site in the east bay hills at the south end of the San Francisco Bay. The site is on the edge of the Santa Clara Valley, adjacent to Silicon Valley, just above the sprawl of the valley floor.
Soil: Loamy clay
USDA Plant Hardiness Zone: 9
Major Plant Materials: *Olea europaea* 'Mission' (Mission olive tree), *Lavandula angustifolia* (English lavender), mustard, barley, and California wildflower seeds
Major Hardscape Materials: Cedar, poured-in-place concrete
Building Description: There are thirteen houses of approximately 4,250 square feet each with a common pool and poolhouse.
Program: Suburban landscaping for a 10-acre site. As a condition of permit approval, no city water was available (well water only) for landscaping.

Below: Landscape site plan by Barbara Stauncher Solomon. **Bottom:** A concept sketch by Solomon. **Right:** A site model.

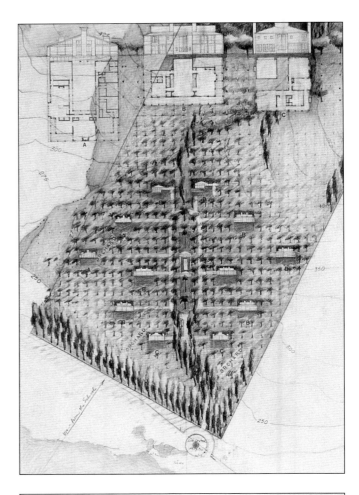

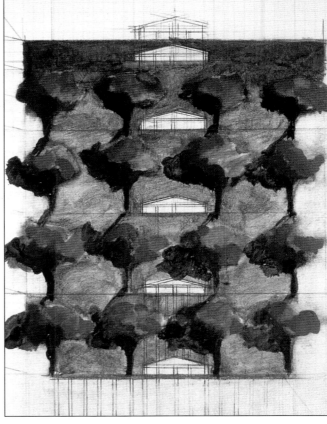

Design

One thousand Mission olive trees are planted 25 feet apart on a barren 10-acre site that was formerly the site of a walnut orchard. They form the structural grid which orders all of the buildings and roads. The access road and driveways fall between the 25-foot grid without interrupting the rhythm of the trees. The tops of the trees, which grow up to 35-feet tall, will eventually reach the eaves of the houses and soften the view from the valley floor.

Lee's Orchard is intended to provide an alternative prototype for low-density suburban development. The landscape is not only extremely efficient in the expenditure of water, fertilizer, and maintenance man-hours, it also has the potential to produce income from the emerging boutique olive oil industry. The olive trees will be managed by the homeowner's association until they begin to bear fruit. The trees, which are of the best olive oil–producing variety, will then be harvested by a local olive oil manufacturer in exchange for the maintenance of the orchard. The olive trees will survive periodic drought without water after the first few years of growth.

CHOMENKO GARDEN

Location: Mill Valley, California
Date of Completion: 1993
Owners: Mary Chomenko and Gregory Hinckley
Landscape Architect: Gary Leonard Strang (GLS)
Design Team: Gary Strang
Consultants: Urban Farmer Store (irrigation)
Photography: Gary Strang
Site Description: A three-quarter acre site in the Marin County hills with a view to the San Francisco Bay, Tiburon, Sausalito, and Angel Island. It is the site of a former ranch, and is subject to summer wind and fog.
Soil: Heavy clay
USDA Plant Hardiness Zone: 9
Major Plant Materials: *Quercus agrifolia* (coast live oak), *Olea europaea 'Mission'* (Mission olive), *Salvia uliginosa*, *Salvia mexicana* (Mexican bush sage), *Stipa gigantea* (giant clump grass), *Festuca californica* (California fescue), *Iris douglasiana* (Pacific Coast iris), wildflower seeds, *Osmanthus fragrans* (sweet olive), apple trees, *Pinus torreyana* (torrey pine), *Myrica californica*.
Major Hardscape Materials: Stained cedar deck, painted cedar trellis and fence, poured-in-place concrete trellis bases, Mexican compost quarry stone, walnut shell mulch.
Building Description: Two-story house.
Program: Completely new landscape with property line fence around entire site, retaining walls.

Design

The street frontage is planted with olive trees and wildflowers which blend with the east bay hills that come up to the curb across the street. The windy front entry yard is planted with closely spaced live oak trees, grasses, and wildflowers. By contrast, the backyard with the view is planted with manicured lawn, sycamore trees, a small apple orchard, a new trellis and deck, and an outdoor stone patio.

The oak forest in the front yard will eventually be a low-maintenance extension of the adjacent natural California landscape.

Gary Leonard Strang is a landscape architect and architect practicing in San Francisco, CA. He specializes in urban and architectural landscapes, and buildings with complex landscape and site planning requirements.

Below: Street view. **Bottom:** Conceptual site plan with wild front entry and manicured backyard with city view.

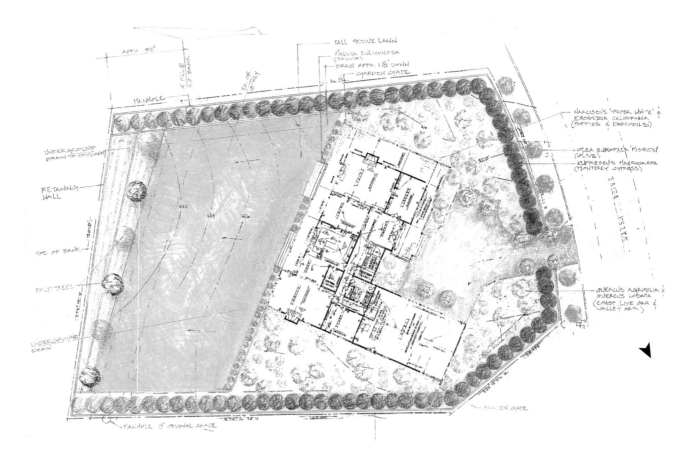

Christine E. Ten Eyck

PARADISE VALLEY RESIDENCE

Location: Paradise Valley, Arizona
Date of Completion: 1995
Owners: Withheld at client's request.
Landscape Architect: The Planning Center
Design Team: Christine Ten Eyck (principal designer, project manager), Susan Damon (assistant production manager)
Architect: Hugh Knoell
General Contractor: McKnight and Barnes General Contractors
Photography: Christine Ten Eyck
Site Description: A small lot, 90 x 90 feet.
Soils: Rocky, alkaline, fast-draining.
USDA Plant Hardiness Zone: 13
Major Plant Materials: Paloverde, ironwood, bear grass.
Major Hardscape Materials: Sandblasted concrete, concrete masonry units, agua marble pool plaster
Lighting: Low-voltage
Building Description: A contemporary remodel of an existing 1950s ranch house on a small site. The architect rebuilt the roof to take advantage of dramatic views of Camelback Mountain to the south.
Program: The challenge in this project was to create a serene retreat on a small property while incorporating a number of features requested by the client.

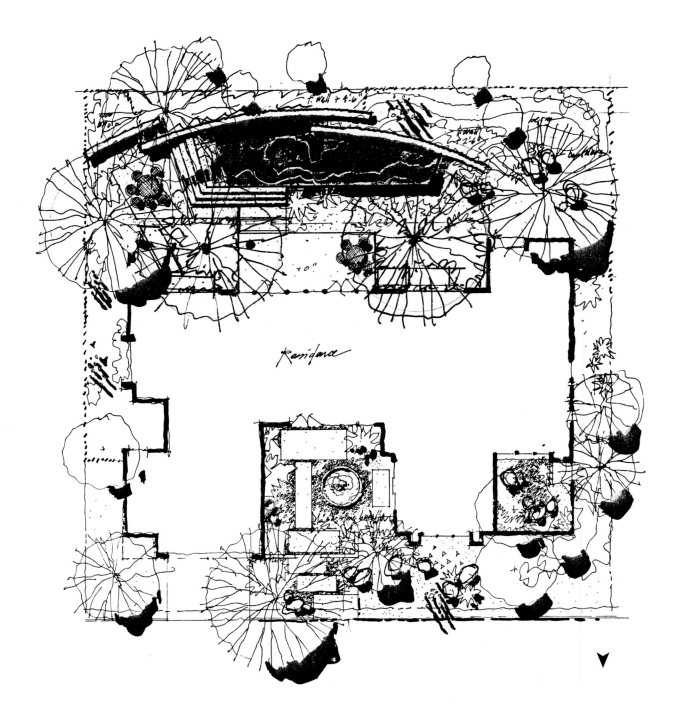

Design

In the front courtyard, sandblasted concrete step pads lead to the entry past a large hand-carved stone bowl fountain. Desert ironwood trees were planted to dip over the fountain. In the back garden, three arcing walls frame the back of a negative-edge pool. Wildflowers and brittlebush tucked in the overlap of two walls are the backdrop for the water that spills from the lowest wall into the pool. The feeling of serenity is heightened by the horizontal foreground of the stepped pool and garden that leads the eye to the dramatic view of Camelback Mountain beyond the desert trees. The horizontal element of the garden is further accentuated by overlapping each course of block on the wall one-half inch forward, creating horizontal shadow patterns along all of the walls.

LEWIS RESIDENCE

Location: Paradise Valley, Arizona
Date of Completion: 1997
Owners: John and Melodie Lewis
Landscape Architect: Floor & Ten Eyck Landscape Architecture, 30 East Northern Avenue, Phoenix, AZ 85020.
Design Team: Christine Ten Eyck (principal designer, project manager), Sarah Wessel (assistant production)
General Contractor: Jeff Franklin
Photography: Richard Maack
Site Description: Sloping site facing west
Soils: Rocky, alkaline, fast-draining
USDA Plant Hardiness Zone: 13
Major Plant Materials: Palo Breas, brittlebush, creosote, chumparosa, goldeneye, Indian fig, prickly pear, green hopbush, desert marigolds
Major Hardscape Materials: Sedona red sandstone, sandblasted cast-in-place concrete, aqua marble deep gray pool plaster
Building Description: An existing Spanish Colonial residence.
Program: The clients wanted a new pool, spa, and entertaining area on a very steeply sloping site. They also required a new front entry and auto court, gates, and a courtyard.

Right: The pool looking north to the hills.

Design

Because of the sloping site, down to an adjacent road on the west, the landscape architect made a series of gently arcing terraced stone gardens and built a half-moon shaped pool into these terraces. The ramada structure was placed between the pool and the street to help with privacy issues. The ramada also serves as another retaining wall to step down to existing grade at the street. (In all, there is a 12-foot drop in elevation.) The landscape architect wanted the pool to feel like an irrigation holding pond in the desert with the concrete flume (that connects the spa and pool) reminiscent of irrigation troughs found in old ranches and farms in Arizona. A wild garden of native lime green Paloverdes, brittlebush, fragrant creosote, and wildflowers surround the pool for a desert riparian swimming experience.

The landscape architect used extremely drought-tolerant plant material, all on drip irrigation.

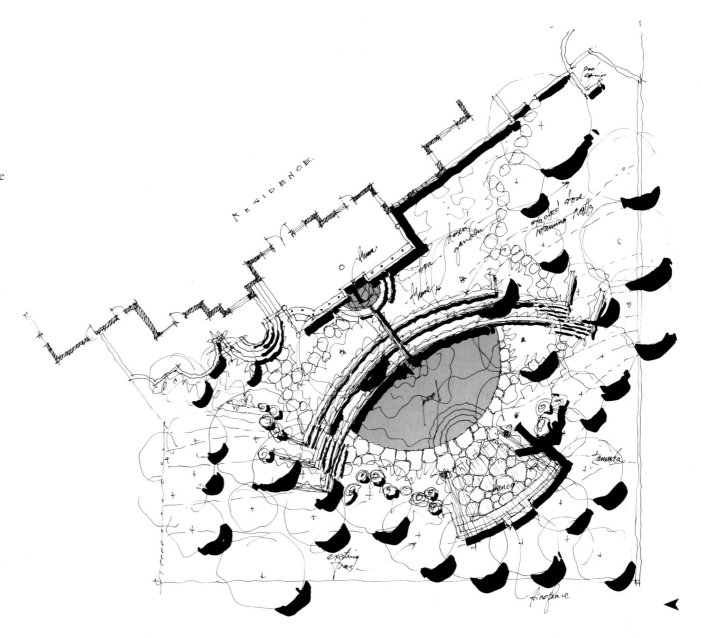

PHOENIX MOUNTAIN PRESERVE RESIDENCE

Location: Phoenix, Arizona
Date of Completion: 1997
Owners: Withheld at client's request.
Landscape Architect: Floor & Ten Eyck Landscape Architecture
Design Team: Christine Ten Eyck (principal designer), Kris Floor
Architect: Hugh Knoell, Knoell Quidort Architects
General Contractor: Schultz Development
Consultants: Tim McQueen (irrigation designer)
Lighting: FX low-voltage
Photography: Richard Maack
Site Description: Rocky, sloping site
Soils: Rocky, alkaline, fast-draining
USDA Plant Hardiness Zone: 13
Major Plant Materials: Ironwood, mesquite, Paloverdes, brittlebush, bursage creosote, chuparosa, desert marigold, prickly pear
Major Hardscape Materials: Sandblasted concrete block, sandblasted cast-in-place concrete, sandblasted salvaged jackhammered concrete
Building Description: Contemporary exposed concrete masonry home with glass and generous overhangs from the inverted "butterfly" metal roof. The architecture takes advantage of mountain preserve views to the south and expansive views to the McDowell Mountains, Pinnacle Peak, and Black Mountain to the north. The house has exposed concrete floors, Douglas fir ceilings, and exposed colored masonry walls.
Program: The client wanted outdoor living spaces, a small pool, fireplace, built-in barbecue, a vegetable garden, and parking for guests.

Right: View of the fireplace and patio looking southeast.

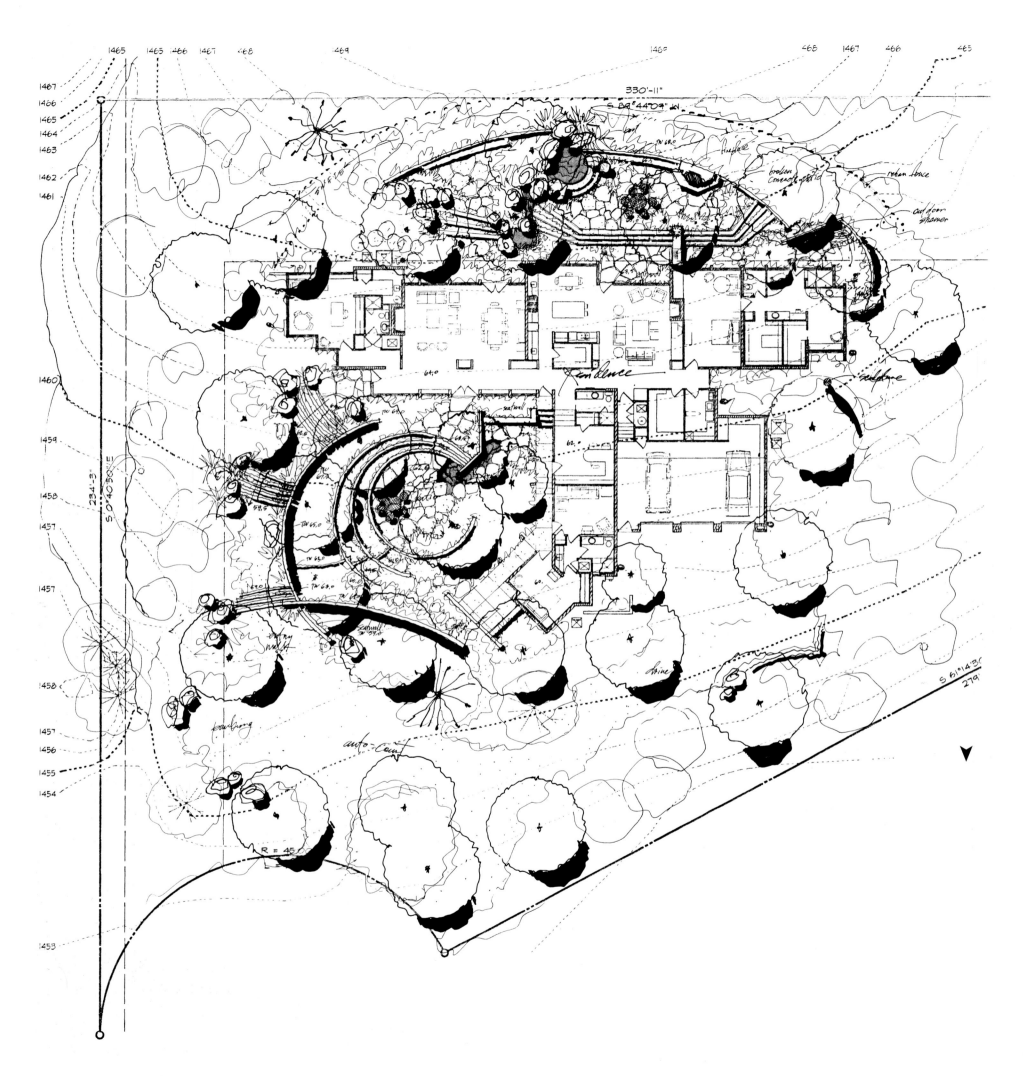

Left: Landscape site plan.
Below: Front courtyard looking south.

Design

The landscape architect used curved concrete masonry walls
to create two courtyards, one on the north side and one on
the south side of the house. Guest parking is tucked into
desert trees in an auto court near the street. The curved
north courtyard wall leads to a series of sandblasted
concrete curb steps with earth between, creating a generous
trail to the front entry with glimpses of the north courtyard
and great views to the mountain preserve to the east. The
north courtyard is formed around a concrete cistern
fountain with raised concentric gardens up to the wall.
Salvaged broken concrete forms the courtyard paving
material that will eventually have creeping plants growing
though it. The south garden features two gently curved
retaining walls. A rock outcropping slips through into a
round swimming pool. Water spills through the boulders
and pool through three runnels into a lower pool. Native
trees and shrubs weave through the garden, attracting a
myriad of desert birds, hummingbirds, and butterflies.

All plants are extremely drought tolerant and are on a drip
irrigation system. The broken concrete for the patio is
recycled. Water is harvested from the roof into the upside-
down culverts that not only double as water features when
it rains but also slow down the water and gently release it
into native seeded revegetated areas and tree wells.

*Christine Ten Eyck received her bachelor of landscape
architecture from Texas Tech University in 1981. Following a
raft trip down the Colorado river thorough the Grand Canyon
in 1985 she was inspired to
move from Texas to Phoenix,
Arizona. In 1995, she started
her own landscape firm, Floor
& Ten Eyck in Phoenix. Her
work currently includes the
Phoenix Indian School Park, a
sensory garden for the visually
impaired, master planning for
The Desert Botanical Garden,
and a number of private
gardens. She resides in Carefree,
Arizona.*

James van Sweden & Wolfgang Oehme

LITTLEFIELD GARDEN

Location: Mohican Hills, Maryland
Date of Completion: 1990
Owner: Dr. Jerald Littlefield
Landscape Architect: Oehme, van Sweden & Associates, Inc., 800 G Street SE, Washington, D.C. 20003
Design Team: James van Sweden, FASLA (principal-in-charge), Sandra Youssef Clinton, ASLA (project manager).
General Contractor: Oehme, van Sweden & Associates, Inc., Birks Company, James Birks (subcontractor)
Photography: James van Sweden
Site Description: Suburban lot of approximately one-quarter acre. House sits high on a hill with views of the Potomac River to the south during the winter months. Neighbors are located closely on either side of the house. Rear garden backs up to a community park providing a lot of borrowed scenery in the rear.
Soils: Heavy clay with boulders of quartz close to the surface
USDA Plant Hardiness Zone: 7
Major Plant Materials: Primarily perennials (*Hypericum calycinum*) and ornamental grasses (*Miscanthus* sp.) with a large *Zelkova serrata* for shade, and a grove of *Betula nigra* 'Heritage' which divides two areas of space in the garden.
Major Hardscape Materials: Pennsylvania bluestone, Stoneyhurst fieldstone
Lighting: Uplights for the trees and low-level garden lights for the planting around the terraces. A built-in lighting system under the coping of the lily pool seat wall lights the terrace just at the edge of the lily pool, making the pool appear to float at night.
Building Description: Very contemporary design with large walls of glass looking out to the rear garden from all floors of the house, which is wood sided and painted, painted steel pipe railings as accents. The kitchen and family room have the prominent views of the garden.
Program: Privacy screening with fence; swimming pool (lap pool); lily pool; play space for one child; retaining walls for major grade breaks between the front and rear garden spaces; storage area for garden and pool equipment.

Below: Water ripples over orange-red stones dug from the site during excavation.
Bottom: Landscape site plan.
Right: A small waterfall is shown on the right. In the foreground a stone bench provides a place to sit close to the water and the fish.

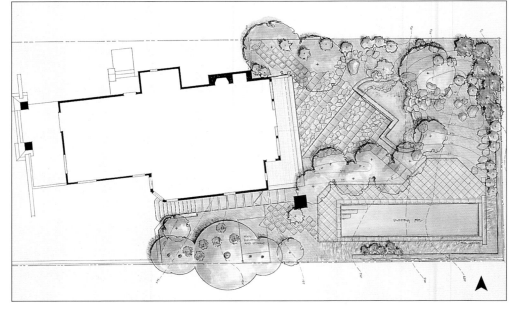

Design

The space limitations in the rear yard began to organize the design of the garden. The pool was placed to the side of the garden and partially screened from view by a grove of river birch so that during the winter months the pool covering was not so obvious. It also allows for more privacy around the pool area. The terrace and lily pool were designed as one piece, on the diagonal, in order to maker a small space appear much larger. Boulders unearthed during house construction were incorporated into the water falls of the lily pool, with the falls facing the main view from the house. The wood fence was designed in a diagonal pattern to enlarge the apparent size of the garden. The view to the park in the rear was left open to increase the length of the overall view from the garden.

This garden is built to last, in hardscape materials selected, construction techniques utilized, and plant selection. Plantings grew to fill the spaces within the first year, giving the garden a mature look. Plants are selected for their toughness, seasonal interest, and ability to withstand years of growth without being divided or transplanted.

MEYER GARDEN

Right: A granite sculpture by Ulrich Ruckreim rises from a "sea" of beach grass and perennials.

Location: Harbert, Michigan
Date of Completion: 1989
Owners: Harriet and Ulrich Meyer
Landscape Architect: Oehme, van Sweden & Associates
Design Team: Wolfgang Oehme, Larry Frank
Landscape Contractor: Gene de la Fore
Photography: James van Sweden
Site Description: Rolling topography, sloping toward Lake Michigan
Soil: Mainly sand
USDA Hardiness Zone: 6
Major Plant Materials: Trees and shrubs: *Pinus sylvestris, Pinus mugo, Pinus nigra, Cornus sericea, Gleditsia triacanthos inermis, Juniperus chinese pfitzeriana, Cotoneaster salicifolius repens, Amelanchier canadensis, Magnolia virginiana, Rosa rugosa, Cornus mas, Ilex verticillata, Potentilla fruticosa;* perennials: *Geranium macrorrhizum, Lysimachia clethroides, Sedum x* 'Herbstfreude,' *Rudbeckia fulgida* 'Goldsturm,' *Persicaria amplexicaulis* 'Firetail,' *Persicaria polymorpha, Persicaria affine, Tanacetum macrophyllum, Ligularia dentata* 'Desdemona,' *Astilbe arendsii, Achillea filipendulina* 'Coronation Gold,' *Lythrum salicaria* 'Morden's Pink,' *Epimedium versicolor* 'Sulphureum,' *Physostegia virginiana* 'Vivid,' *Eryngium yuccifolium, Salvia nemorosa* 'Ostfriesland,' *Veronica spicata* 'Sunny Border Blue'; grasses and bamboo: *Pennisetum alopecuroides, Panicum virgatum* 'Haense Herms,' *Miscanthus sinensis giganteus, Miscanthus sinensis* 'Malepartus,' *Ammophila breviligulata, Molinia litorialis* 'Windspiel,' *Fargesia murielae*
Major Hardscape Materials: Concrete driveway, wood boardwalks and decks, asphalt tennis court
Building Description: Modern in the Bauhaus style, with large windows overlooking Lake Michigan.
Program: The client's wife experienced an Oehme, van Sweden garden in Baltimore, Maryland, at her aunt's house and wanted a similar garden for her own house. She particularly liked the ornamental grasses and perennials and she wanted large areas devoted to them. Consequently, there is no lawn area, although there are paths throughout as wooden boardwalks or mulch. The landscape architects used perennials for different seasons.

Design

The tennis court area was planted with large groups of *Miscanthus giganteus*, pinus, and cornus to screen and soften. There are several sculptures placed throughout the garden and a setting of different plantings was provided for each. There is enough plant variety (trees, shrubs, perennials, grasses, bulbs) to provide interest throughout the year. The dried leaves and flowerstalks remain all winter. They are cut down and mulched only when the daffodils appear in the spring. Because of the sandy soil, soil tests are made on a regular basis to determine fertilizer needs. Weeding is done on a regular basis by a landscape contractor who did the original planting. The landscape architects selected plants that grow with a minimum of care and have a long blooming period.

MINTZ GARDEN

Location: Capital Hill, Washington, District of Columbia
Date of Completion: 1994
Owner: Dr. Gary Mintz
Landscape Architect: Oehme, van Sweden & Associates, Inc.
Design Team: James van Sweden, FASLA (principal-in-charge), Wolfgang Oehme, FASLA (planting design), Eric Groft, ASLA (project manager)
Architect: Michael Hauptman, Brawer & Hauptman, Philadelphia, PA
General Contractor: Tom Glass, Washington, D.C., Oehme, van Sweden & Associates (landscape contractor), Tom Sites, Gardens of Earth, Luray, VA (subcontractor).
Consultant: Dr. Frank Gouin (soils consultant)
Photography: James van Sweden
Site Description: Urban street corner in a residential neighborhood. The building is sited on the property line abutting the neighboring house on one side and an alley and streets on the other sides. The design consists of a front entry garden and a side/rear terrace garden.
Soils: Urban fill. The site had been paved with concrete since 1910. The sub-grade was fill from the building's original construction. There were toxic levels of several trace minerals (magnesium, calcium). The unusable course material was removed, the remaining soil was treated with pyrite sulfur, and new topsoil and amendments were incorporated into the soil.
USDA Plant Hardiness Zone: 7
Major Plant Materials: *Ilex x attenuata* 'Fosteri' and *Ilex pedunculosa* for screening; *Cornus kousa,* stewartia, hamamelis, *Cornus mas* for specimen deciduous trees; mahonia, fothergilla, and nandina for shrub massings and low-level vertical accent; rudbeckia, *Hakoneckchloa* sp., carex, imperata, *Panicum virgatum* 'Heavy metal,' *Hosta sieboldiana, Astilbe japonica* 'Deutschland,' and stachys dominate the ground plane in the sunny terrace garden that is punctuated with *Molinia littorailis* 'Windspeil' as the vertical specimen grass.

The front entry garden, which is shady, includes *Geranium macrorrhizum*, helleborus, *Rodgersia* sp., *Acanthus* sp., tiarella, and *Hosta* spp. The spring bulbs include the old favorites: naturalized daffodils and lily flowering tulips along with a collection of exotic specimens which the owner has collected over the years.

Right: The garden seen from the public sidewalk. A sculpture by George Rickey and a large ceramic cone by Paul Chaleff contrast sharply with soft perennial plantings.

Major Hardscape Materials: Pennsylvania bluestone terraces, black wrought iron fencing with ball finials

Lighting: A tall garden lantern provides lighting at the entry garden, and similarly designed bollard lights are placed symmetrically on either side of the old front entrance to the building. Small spotlights highlight specimen plant materials as well as the client's sculpture collection.

Building Description: A turn of the century traditional bank building with limestone veneer and carved limestone pediment and detailing. The building served as a bank until the 1980s and then was remodeled and converted into a residence.

Program: The side door of the building became the front door and the ceremonial front door became the door to the terrace garden. The design objective was to provide a clear distinction between the two doors. A small outdoor seating area with privacy was the main objective for the body of the garden. The entry garden announces the entrance and provides an outdoor storage area and parking for one car.

Design

The garden was designed to fit within the context of the historic neighborhood and the building's stately architecture while fulfilling the client's need for a cutting-edge garden to accommodate his contemporary sculpture collection and the modern interior spaces. The entry consists of a "carpet" of square cut bluestone set on a diagonal with a broad border of rectangular cut bluestone. Concrete cobbles pave the designated off-street parking space. A finely designed and crafted wood storage cabinet features tongue-and-groove siding and a standing seam copper roof to house garbage and garden tools.

A black wrought iron gate provides access into the fenced side and back terrace garden. Stepping stones lead along the side of the bank to the old front where the outdoor terrace is located.

A square terrace is set at a slight angle to the building and reflects the rotated grid of the interior spaces and provides an area for outdoor dining or sitting. A rough border of brown bluestone frames a field of square smooth bluestone. Several pieces of contemporary sculpture are placed either on or around the terrace. Lush plantings surround the garden and provide four seasons of viewing pleasure when viewed from the terrace or through the double doors of the living room.

WOODWARD GARDEN

Location: Georgetown, Washington, District of Columbia
Date of Completion: 1991
Owner: Barbara Bolling Woodward
Landscape Architect: Oehme, van Sweden & Associates, Inc.
Design Team: James van Sweden, FASLA (principal-in-charge), Sandra Youssef Clinton, ASLA (project manager)
General Contractor: Oehme, van Sweden & Associates, Inc., Birks Company, James Birks (water feature installation and terrace installation), Stone Forest (granite stone fountain carving), Hannan and Lerner (cabinetmakers)
Photography: James van Sweden
Site Description: Very long and narrow city lot, 17 x 80 feet. Enclosed on all sides by wood fences. Garden is on the north side of the house.
Soils: Space had been previously gardened so soil was rich with organic material.
USDA Plant Hardiness Zone: 7
Major Plant Materials: Primarily perennials, shrubs, and trees. Many wet-loving plants near the fountain (*Iris* sp.), and shade-loving plants due to heavy shade from overhanging flowering cherry and neighbor's trees. Shade plants include hosta, astilbe, liriope.
Major Hardscape Materials: Pennsylvania bluestone terrace with fieldstone and gravel inset, fieldstone stepping stones
Lighting: Uplights for the trees and low-level garden lights for the planting around the terraces.
Building Description: Historic Georgetown brick house in a neighborhood of similar houses. The garden area takes up the entire rear yard and is viewed very prominently from the family room of the house.
Program: Privacy screening with fence; water feature; access to the rear of the garden space; counter with built-in cabinets for buffet use; terrace for small seating area; seasonal changes in plant material for an all-season garden.

Right: A pink granite fountain, seen here in the summer, is placed midway along a dry stream of stone.

Design

There is a Japanese spirit to this garden. The use of different stone types with a dry stream of rock imbedded into the terrace evoke details from Japanese gardens. The custom-designed granite fountain spiraling from the top center out to the rim of the fountain provides a focal point from the house and the terrace. Lush plantings screen views of the rear areas of the garden, however the stepping stones draw the viewer into its depth.

This garden is built to last, in terms of hardscape materials selected, construction techniques utilized, and plant selection. Plantings grew to fill the spaces within the first year, giving the garden a mature look. They are selected for their toughness, seasonal interest, and ability to withstand years of growth without being divided or transplanted.

James van Sweden and Wolfgang Oehme founded the firm of Oehme, van Sweden & Associates in 1977. Since then, they have collaborated on a full range of landscape design projects,

may of which have been honored with distinguished awards and published reviews. Mr. van Sweden's latest book, Gardening with Water: How James van Sweden and Wolfgang Oehme Build and Plant Fountains, Swimming Pools, Lily Pools, Ponds, and Water Edges *(1995) is the first in a series of garden books for Random House.*

H. Keith Wagner

HILLTOP RESIDENCE

Location: New England
Date of Completion: 1996
Owners: Withheld at client's request.
Landscape Architect: Office of H. Keith Wagner, 504 A Dalton Drive, Colchester, Vermont 05446
Design Team: H. Keith Wagner (principal), Lisa Delplace (associate project landscape architect), Aaron Stein (associate)
Architect: Truex Cullins and Partners
General Contractor: 3 Seasons Builders
Landscape Contractor: Landmark Landscaping
Photography: H. Keith Wagner
Site Description: One-hundred acre hillside
Soils: Well-drained glacial till with ledge outcroppings
USDA Plant Hardiness Zone: 4
Major Plant Materials: Moss, fern, birch, maple, hemlock
Major Hardscape Materials: Panton stone, stone walls from the site
Program: The home was new residential construction. The 100-acre site, selected by the client, is a microcosm of the New England state in which it is located: dramatic vistas, pristine vegetation, and inherently quiet. The client requested a comprehensive landscape design that would wed landscape to the architecture.

Design

In response to the poetic nature of the site, the haiku poetry of the Japanese poet Basho was selected as a guiding design principle. His poem "The Hilltop Temple" provided a sensory metaphor for both the ascending journey to the site and the site itself. This was expressed in simple bold gestures through geometry and rhythm which derived their cadence from the architecture and the site's axial forces.

Taking cues from the site, the geometry of the vernacular fieldstone walls is echoed in the design as stone bands providing axial datum lines. Materials for the composition were selected based on their individual intrinsic beauty and their overall contribution to the design. A simple yet bold palette of indigenous plants and construction materials was used, each selected for the subtle variation in hue and texture.

The judicious use of light and shadow was an extremely important design element. A canopy of seventeen white birch, reflecting the structure and the syllables in a haiku poem, mingle with the existing canopy of sugar maples and oaks, proving a dappled sense of enclosure. A long band of

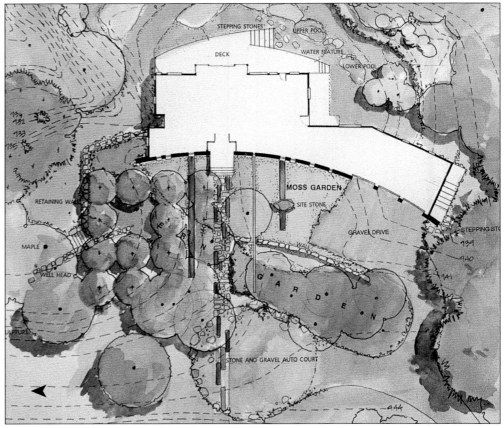

Top left: View of the moss garden looking towards the birch grove. **Bottom left:** Landscape site plan. **Right:** View of the light trough.

enter into light
birch grove.

cut panton stone emulates the site datum and is placed in a composition of gravel, fieldstone, and native fern. In addition, a fifty-two foot trough of light, reflects a narrow aperture in the stone facade of the house. Reflective by day, the trough richly bisects and unifies the spaces at night with a gentle wash of warm light.

H. Keith Wagner, ASLA, is a Burlington, VT–based landscape architect whose work encompasses all fields of design ranging in scale from the master plan to site design, products, and sculpture. Wagner studied at Syracuse University-SUNY School of Landscape Architecture. In 1989 he formed The Office of H.

Keith Wagner, a firm whose approach and vision to landscape architecture is underlined by the philosophy that landscape architecture is an art form and built forms are sculpture in the landscape. His concerns are those of an artist: how one perceives, approaches, and engages in the sculptural spaces.

Morgan Wheelock

OCEANFRONT RETREAT

Location: Palm Beach, Florida
Date of Completion: 1989
Owners: Withheld at client's request.
Landscape Architects: Morgan Wheelock Incorporated/ Wheelock, Sanchez & Maddux, 362 Summer Street, Summerville, MA 02144; 235 Peruyian Avenue, Palm Beach, FL 33480
Design Team: Morgan Wheelock (principal)
Architect: Jack Train Associates, Betsy Train (architect)
Consultants: Betsy Train Interiors
Photography: Morgan Wheelock, Incorporated
Site Description: Ocean front acre just behind a primary dune on the Atlantic Ocean
Soils: Primary sand dune
USDA Plant Hardiness Zone: 10B
Major Plant Materials: Cabbage palm, pittospourm, scavola, seagrape, ginger, crinum lily, bougainvillea
Major Hardscape Material: Coquina coral stone
Building description: One story and loft complex of three structures built around a pompeian courtyard surrounded by a colonnade and enclosed by a walled and gated perimeter.
Program: Intellectually, the program was to provide the antithesis of a Northeast "English" garden—to provide a sense of tropical jungle. Juxtaposed was the client's desire to achieve a sense of cloistered contemplation and purity of thought against the background of raging jungle and pounding Atlantic surf.

Design

Due to relentless ocean winds, most outdoor living takes place behind the house in the protected courtyard. Thus, the focus is the central courtyard, executed as pure architecturally cloistered space. Yet this onesided, limited characterization of pure thought is inadequate for a wholly integrated human existence. Therefore, the design slices through the apparent security of the courtyard and invites the eye to travel along corridors and axes which ultimately

thrust the mind into the natural "jungle" landscape. The integration of cerebral and natural is induced through design. The completed project balances the realm of pure intellect—pure control—with ever changing, never controlled processes of nature. This is accomplished visually and functionally since all access to and from the house is on the natural vectors.

As with all designs in hostile environments, the Atlantic coast being one, what survives is what has naturalized to the adverse conditions. The design uses bold, natural material in strong masses and creates design structure through reassembling random natural survivors into blocks and formats which organize and support the spatial design.

COLLECTOR'S TOWN HOUSE

Location: Washington, District of Columbia
Date of Completion: 1988
Owners: Withheld at client's request.
Landscape Architect: Morgan Wheelock, Inc.
Design Team: Morgan Wheelock (principal), Keith LeBlanc (associate)
Architect: Hartman and Cox Architects
General Contractor: E.A. Baker
Landscape Contractor: Thomas E. Carroll & Son
Consultant: Olympic Pool Company
Photography: Morgan Wheelock, Inc.
Site Description: Urban site adjacent to Rock Creek Park
USDA Plant Hardiness Zone: 7
Major Plant Materials: Magnolia, cherry, dogwood, viburnum, camellia, hydrangea
Major Hardscape Materials: Limestone, Atlantic green granite (pool)
Building Description: A 4-story Georgian mansion
Program: The program called for a swimming pool and formal entertainment spaces relating to indoor assembly areas.

Design

The mansion towers over the garden to the extent that the size of the garden is falsely diminished. Thus, great effort was taken to enlarge the apparent scale of the garden so that it might balance with the scale of the house. A tiled pool was built on axis with the grand ballroom with its sides subtly canted to a vanishing point. The effect is to visually lengthen the garden by almost 50 percent. The counter axis through the center of the pool was also extended by creating a wide window opening in the enclosing wall. This extends the view across a public street into the canopies of trees in Rock Creek Park. The owners' sculpture was sited in the garden to emphasize the system of axes and view corridors, effectively expanding the sense of space.

Plants inside the walled garden were matched with plants outside where the design called for visual extension, while contrasting plant material (magnolias) against neighboring sycamore and maple was used to screen views of adjacent houses. The garden borrows its view from adjacent properties, frequently losing the sense of its own enclosure.

Below: The garden. **Bottom:** Landscape site plan. **Right:** The pool. **Far right:** Descent into the garden.

Morgan Wheelock, president and founder of the firm bearing his name, has practiced landscape architecture since 1964, and is registered in ten states. In 1988, he was elected a Fellow of the ASLA for design excellence in completed work. In addition to professional practice, he has been active on education and advisory committees for Harvard University. He has served on numerous design juries and professional panels on design. Currently he is chairman of the Design Advisory Committee for the National Garden in Washington, DC.

Ron Wigginton

NAPA VALLEY RESIDENCE

Location: Rutherford, California

Date of Completion: 1995

Owners: Withheld at client's request.

Landscape Architect: Ron Wigginton, Land Studio, 733 Allston Way, Berkeley, California 94710

Design Team: Ron Wigginton, Susan Herrington

Architect: Michael Guthrie, Guthrie/Friedlander

General Contractor: James Noland Construction, Inc.

Consultants: Jerry Berg (olive trees), Scott and Barbara Reinsimar (post-construction phase two plant design), Bartelt Engineering

Photography: Ron Wigginton/Land Studio

Site Description: Napa Valley hillside with views across the valley to wineries and a distant view to the San Francisco Bay. Native oak stands and pre-existing rough grading adapted to new residential building program by the architect and landscape architect.

USDA Plant Hardiness Zone: 8

Major Plant Materials: Native and adapted drought-tolerant plants. *Quercus agrifolia, Eucalyptus citriodora, Olea* 'Picateen Orchard,' *Platanus acerifolia* 'Bloodgood,' *Pyrus cymmunis*, grape vineyard, *Ceanothus* ssp., *Heteromeles arbutifolia*, salvia, rosmarinus, *Rhamnus californica*, cistus, *Dietes vegeta, Lavandula augustifolia,* iris, *Artemesia* ssp., santolina, meadow grass, and wildflower hydroseed mixes, water-loving plants for "bog garden"—nymphaea, *Equisetum hyemale, Nelumbo lutea*

Major Hardscape Materials: Texas limestone walls and deck surfaces, decomposed "Yosemite gold" granite walking and driving surfaces, bronze and wood gates, custom steel edging, and concentric "rock rings"

Building Description: A new residential stone hillside complex with vineyard and olive orchard. Single-family home with separate guest, caretaker quarters, and garages, linear trellis, potting, and tool buildings forming a large circle around a central circular drivecourt. A lower walking terrace and retaining walls connect a stone-edged swimming pool, tennis court, formal raised vegetable garden, and agricultural/winery building, to form a secondary ring.

Program: An out-of-state family wanted to build a second home to be close to their expanding business in California. The landscape and building design integrate the company business through agricultural imagery and through the production of olive oil and wine on the site. The arrangement of buildings and terraces maximizes distant views and extends the use of the hillside. The pool, spa, and tennis court are created with stone and wood to minimize visual impact and are in keeping with the Napa Valley vernacular.

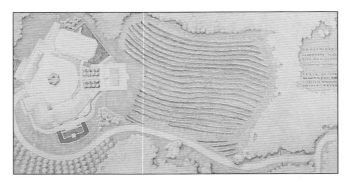

Right: Hillside phase two
planting under oak trees.
Below right: Circular drive
court of decomposed granite
with steel edging at the main
house.

Design

The landscape architect worked with the architect at the
early site design stage to ameliorate a previous owner's
program and rough grading. In some instances, the
problems presented by the previous earthwork were
capitalized on. In one instance, the incorrect solar
orientation of the unbuilt tennis court play area was left as a
large grass "shadow" that contained and defined the new
and correctly rotated court. The entry road was realigned
slightly to create strong view lines while the landscape
design created a well-defined sequence of contrasting native
and agricultural zones.

The circular drive court design was reinforced by
amplifying its geometry to include a lower secondary terrace
that linked the winery and swimming pool. The center
point of the drive court was used to create radial lines that
defined the layout of the olive orchard rows. This large "fan"
of two-hundred mature olive trees became the "Radial
Orchard" and one of the main drive-through features of the
estate. The forced perspective taper of the raised stone wall
of the vegetable garden also plays off this organizing
concept. A highly detailed inner court with buildings
arranged in a circle gives way to informal landscape as one
moves downhill away from the residence. Spaces between
five stone buildings such as the sycamore forecourt create a
secondary entry to the winery building. Low stone
seat/walls in this area form an outdoor reception and eating
area. It is augmented by an outdoor fire pit and a fireplace
with movable furniture. Descending to the lower terraces,
one walks among a fragrant checkerboard of rosemary and
lavender. These broad curving terraces lead to the stone
swimming pool deck directly below the house's formal stone
terrace. Broad stone stairs lead down into the pool with its
in-water seating and unobstructed view. Designed with a
unique high-level waterline, the surface acts as a reflecting
pool and a foreground for the long valley view to San
Francisco Bay.

Native and self-sustaining (drought-tolerant) plant material
was utilized. Trees control west setting sun and offer some
shade control.

Above: Sycamore forecourt leading to the agricultural building from the central drive court. **Above right:** Stone-edged pool surrounded by a lawn panel at the terrace below the main house. **Right:** View towards the main house from the agricultural building.

RITCHKEN RESIDENCE

Location: Del Mar, California
Date of Completion: 1989
Owners: Simon and Debra Ritchken
Landscape Architect: Ron Wigginton/Land Studio
Design Team: Ron Wigginton, Rachada Chantaviriyavit, Scott Molentin, Caroline Lee (phase two)
Architect: John Nalevanko
General Contractor: Benchmark Landscape Construction
Photography: Ron Wigginton/Land Studio
Site Description: Existing single-family residence on a coastal California lot
Major Plant Materials: Relocation of existing on-site pines, palms, and cycads *Bauhinia blakeliana, Lagerstroemia indica, Pittosporum tobira* 'Wheelers Dwarf,' *Fragaria chiloensis, Strelitzia reginae, Hibiscus rosa-sinensis,* sod lawn
Major Hardscape Materials: Integral color sandblasted concrete walls, steps, pads, and curved walks, painted redwood decking, painted redwood, metal gates, and Nalevanko chairs and sofa.
Lighting: Multiple "Starlights" set into walls at "shotgun" entry stairway.
Building Description: Modern Southern California wood and glass residence. New circular family room added to end of residence in conjunction with a new landscape renovation.
Program: Renovation of front and side yards, and second phase landscape entry. Family with young children needed to expand residence and outdoor play and formal areas. New landscape elements created to formalize and identify entry. Flat sod areas were needed for children's play area.

Design

The landscape architect mimicked the circular form of the new building addition to create a "pond ripple" landscape of concentric ring walkways in grass. The elegant ripple walkways also serve as children's toy highways. Walks terminate in small stairs set into a profuse flower bank for child-size seating under the "roof" of large existing pine. The front entry is connected to the street by a long staircase with contemporary fittings and lighting.

The addition of a low containing wall and gates adds security to the area, while visual continuity remains unbroken at the integral front entry. The low gate at street level opens to a tall funnel stairway. Stars illuminate the climb at night. The top of the stairs opens to a formal grass seating terrace which showcases two sculptural chairs on rotated square bases. The terrace offers a view towards the Pacific Ocean before arriving at the new porch and front door. The second low gate to the right opens to the large concentric "pond ripple" garden contained within a smooth stucco wall.

Right: Terrace overlook by the front door to the residence.

Plant material was chosen to control the setting sun and offer some shade control while facilitating or framing filtered ocean views. New trees will sequentially serve as main trees when existing pines need replacement. Specialized and non-drought plant material is contained within special compact areas and in the shade of larger trees.

Above: Circular garden paths leading to the children's step seats under the existing pine tree. **Right, clockwise from top left:** Circular garden paths looking towards the entry gate at the side yard; Nalevanko sofa on the circular patio with garden paths; view from the side yard through the gate to the front door terrace over-look; Nalevanko chairs on terrace overlook at the front door.

Ron Wigginton has lectured on the meaning of the landscape in conjunction with his built work at Harvard University's Graduate School of Design, Stanford University, and the

University of California at Davis and at Berkeley, where Land Studio is located. In 1991, Mr. Wigginton was the first landscape architect to be appointed a Resident Fellow at the University of California's Humanities Research Institute. His work has been published nationally and internationally. He was awarded an Individual Grant for Design Innovation by the national Endowment for the Arts in 1993.

John L. Wong

NAGELBERG RESIDENCE

Location: Ventura County, California
Date of Completion: 1994
Owners: Dr. Steve and Mrs. Jerry Nagelberg
Landscape Architect: John L. Wong, The SWA Group, 22000 Bridgeway Boulevard, Sausalito, CA 94966
Design Team: John L. Wong, John Loomis
Architect: Michael C. F. Chan and Associates, Los Angeles, CA
General Contractor: Bill Pollin
Consultants: Ron Ribbers-ISC (fountain), Rick Samson (irrigation)
Photography: Tom Fox, The SWA Group
Site Description: One and three-quarters acres of flat ground in a triangular lot on a ridge. The unvegetated site abuts neighbors on two sides with views to a golf course and a distant hill on the third side.
Soil: Hillside
USDA Plant Hardiness Zone: 20, 21
Major Plant Materials: Coast live oak, California pepper, American sweetgum, sycamore, pine, pear, plum trees, mixed perennials, native wildflowers, grass
Major Hardscape Materials: Stone cobble, precast concrete paver, light sandblasted concrete, tile
Lighting: Path lights, tree uplights, tree downlights, and accent lights for water features.
Building Description: Primarily a one-story building with concrete tile roof. Various shades of warm earth-tone plaster combine with variations of stone cladding. A series of pavilions and rooms juxtaposed and connected by an internal hallway loop, and are organized to evoke a hill town.
Program: The client requested multiple areas inside and outside for private events and to entertain family and guests in an innovative, unique, and modern setting. They wanted a one-story house with maximum privacy and views; a variety of water features; a swimming pool with spa; a large lawn area for informal games; and adequate screening of two adjacent neighbors.

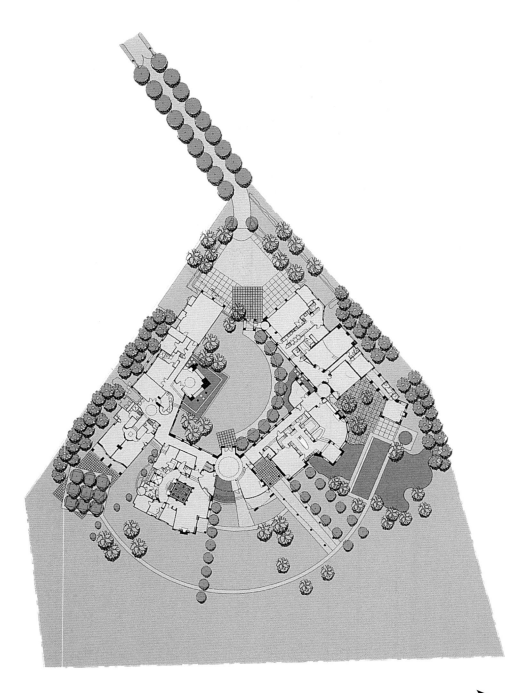

➤

Left: Landscape site plan.
Right: View of the pool house and spa garden from the cut flower garden where ginger, lilies, day lilies, lavenders, foxgloves, bell flowers, gardenias, and marguerites are grown.

Left, clockwise from top: A terrace in lawn parterre extends around the pool, spa, and cut flower garden; connecting to the family room and kitchen, the breakfast room is located in a square pavilion, the dark-bottom swimming pool "floats" in a pond, and water elevation is set at seating height in relation to the breakfast room; view of the round foyer/rotunda with an interior water wall casting water into a water stair, with the water continuing to flow out to the garden and connect to the hillside beyond. **Right:** A forced perspective view of the golf course and surrounding hillside, seen from the gallery, interior court yard, and music room.

Design

The design was a close collaboration among the landscape architect, the architect, and the client. The building and landscape are integrated as one idea, offering excitement with some surprises.

There are a series of different indoor and outdoor spaces connected by an internal hallway loop and an exterior pathway loop, organized into a circular form that defines an internal courtyard and an external view–oriented garden room. Careful juxtaposition of rooms, openings, and windows creates a view corridor that links the interior living areas with garden areas inside and outside the circular building cluster. Eight major and minor view axes are framed either by the room and window layout or by the layout of landscape elements of stones, paving, pots, and plantings. Water is used selectively to delight, refresh, and charm the users. Five water features knit together the indoor and outdoor spaces: a greenhouse/parlor water stair into a lily pool; a reflecting pool surrounding the music room; a water wall and fountain stair in the foyer; a jet fountain in the master bedroom; and a swimming pool/spa set in a larger garden pond with fountains.

Except for the grass area, emphasis is on low maintenance.

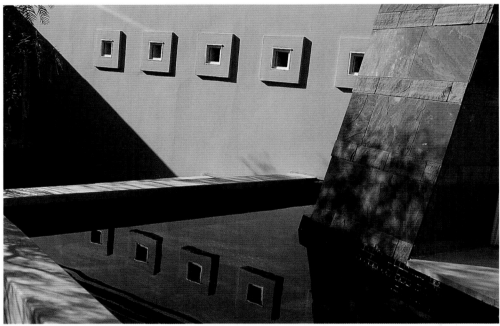

Top left: The music room commands an important location for the complex. Clad with rough reddish stone, the pavilion is floated on a reflecting pool. The opening is sited on axis with the front entrance portal on one side, with the view of the exterior through the gallery and court garden on the second side, and terminating the gallery on the third side. **Center left:** Reflection of the music room and architectural details. **Bottom left:** Stepping-stones float and connect to the entrance of the music room. **Right:** An allée of American sweetgum sweeps in front of the greenhouse/parlor that, anchored by the vertical water stairs, forms the backdrop for the interior lawn court.

COLLECTOR'S RESIDENCE

Location: Southern California
Date of Completion: 1997
Owners: Withheld at client's request.
Landscape Architect: John L. Wong, The SWA Group
Design Team: John L. Wong, John S. Loomis, Maureen Simmons, Rene Bihan, William Blossom
Architect: Michael C. F. Chan and Associates, Los Angeles, CA
General Contractor: ORO Construction
Consultants: Ron Ribbers-ISC (fountain), Rick Samson (irrigation)
Photography: Tom Fox, The SWA Group
Site Description: Flat lot in an established residential neighborhood.
Soils: Amended per the existing conditions
USDA Plant Hardiness Zone: 22, 23
Major Plant Materials: Coast live oak, European white birch, ficus, olive, Italian cypress, carrotwood trees, privet, boxwood, mixed perennials, grass
Major Hardscape Materials: Limestone, granite cobble, decomposed granite
Lighting: Path light, tree uplights, tree downlights, accent light for water features and artworks
Building Description: A French limestone house with traditional classic period architectural details. The building is two stories with garage in basement. In addition to the formal layout of the main house, a pool house and a guardhouse form the residential complex.
Program: Design a garden that respects the formal layout of the main residence and accommodates the display of a private collection of Rodin bronze sculptures.

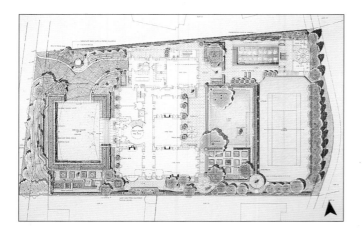

Right: Paved with limestone, the grand terrace is framed by a multi-trunk California live oak and a rusty leaf fig tree. The great lawn is edged by a decomposed granite band. Auguste Rodin's *Eustache De Sainte Pierre, Vetu* is sited on axis with the gallery and terrace room on the left. On the right, *The Three Shades* is centered on axis with the opening of the central garden room, aligning with the grand rotunda and front entry.
Below: Landscape site plan.

Above: Auguste Rodin's *Jean D'Aire, Nude* in the foreground and *The Spirit of Eternal Repose with Head* in the back anchor the garden on the side. Clipped green gems contrast with the bronze railing that edges drifts of camellias and evergreens. These form the connection between the two pieces of art. All the artwork has lighting from above and below. **Above right:** In the center, Rodin's *Seated Woman—Cybele* becomes a part of the overall composition within the parterre garden.

Above left: A hybrid 'Coral Pink' climbing tea rose will eventually punctuate the vine lattice to form the backdrop for Georg Kolbe's *Grosse Sitzende*. Red flowering hibiscus and camellias are planted in the openings for special effect. **Above:** Enzo Plazzotta's *Jamican Girl*, placed in the sunken garden complement the water feature and vine latticework in the stone niche.

Design

With simplicity and timeless and understated elegance, the design consists of a series of garden rooms extending the house's formal layout of interior rooms. An outdoor gallery was designed for the Rodin artworks. Throughout the design process, there was a close collaboration among the landscape architect, the architect, the contractor and subcontractors, and the clients.

There is an arrival court garden paved with stone cobbles and clipped ficus trees and hedges; a secret garden of herbs and color display; a sunken garden court with fountain jets and vine latticework; a big lawn garden with the grand terrace; a parterre garden with seasonal colors; a library garden; a pool garden with vine latticework; and a recreation court garden.

John L. Wong is the managing principal and a design principal for The SWA Group in Sausalito, CA. He is a graduate of landscape architecture and urban design from the University of

California, Berkeley and Harvard University and is the recipient of the Rome Prize in Landscape Architecture from the American Academy in Rome. Project experiences range from major public mixed use and corporate and campus facilities to recreational and resort projects as well as residential gardens in the United States and abroad.

Top right: The parterre garden room is on axis with the view from the terrace off the grand salon. **Center right:** Cross axis with steps leading to the pool garden terrace, as viewed from the great lawn. **Bottom right:** A view of the pool house from the terrace of the grand salon. **Far right, clockwise from top**: Paved with academy black granite cobble, the arrival garden court forms the base for the front entrance facade. Next is a view of the pool garden with sixteen jets set against the pool house. Lastly, a view of the recreation court garden from the upper terrace overlook. Painted wood lattice and forced perspective trompe-l'oeils provide the surface accent treatment to the lower court garden walls.

Index